THE BED SKETCH BOOK

Wendy Baker

an imprint of Morris Genealogical Books SA
Grans-près-Céligny, Switzerland

Wendy Baker's
Interior Design Team

The Old Malthouse
Ham
Marlborough
Wiltshire SN8 3RB
Telephone 01488 66 8989
Fax 01488 66 8818

London
Telephone 0171 381 1515
Fax 0171 610 1882

Other Books by Wendy Baker

THE CURTAIN SKETCH BOOK

Sketches by
Chrissie Carriere

Published in 1995 in the original version
by Deco Books
an imprint of Morris Genealogical Books SA
Rue du Bugnon 7, 1299 Crans-près-Céligny
Switzerland
Tel: (41-22) 776 81 90
Fax: (41-22) 776 08 89
ISBN 2-88046-269-X

Printed by ProVision Pte Ltd in Singapore
Tel: (0065) 334 7720 Fax: (0065) 334 7721
Manufactured in Singapore by Teck Wah Paper Products Ltd

First printing, 1995

1 2 3 4 5 6 7 8 9 / 02 01 00 99 98 97 96 95 94

Contents

A Dream Come True

About one third of our lives are spent in bed, so whilst there, we might as well enjoy our surroundings. As a child, bed is a warm, comforting place that is shared with one's best friends, teddy or perhaps a doll. We therefore, for the rest of our lives, enjoy the comfort, security and joy that bed provides, whether it be with teddy or perhaps someone else.

We all have images of how beds should be. A grand country house will have a four poster with monogrammed linen, and be so large that it could accomodate the whole family. A cottage in the country will have an old iron bedstead with a thick mattress on rickety springs with the crispest of white sheets that smell of clean fresh air after being aired outside in the morning sun, and perhaps providing the best night's sleep for many a day. We should therefore create the most comfortable beds in our own homes where our children can feel safe and snug and our guests rather grand.

***Wendy Baker** has gathered together in this book lots of ideas to enable you to choose your ideal bed. If you have a limited budget, buy the simplest of beds and be daring with your bed linen and covers. Mix prints, plains and stripes together to give a fabulous effect. It is surprisingly easy to create the bed of your dreams, and perhaps this book will start you off in the right direction.*

General Hints

1. *Your bed should be manufactured by a well known and reputable company. (See list at back of book).*

2. *Buy the most expensive bed you can afford. It will last longer than a cheap bed and be kinder to your back.*

3. *If you and your partner have different needs regarding a mattress, most good bedding stores are prepared to supply a combination of soft and hard mattresses which can be zipped together. Reylon and Vi-Spring are recommended for this type of bed.*

4. *When buying a bed, visit a good bedding centre or department store that has trained staff to assist you with your choice. Don't forget to lay on the bed before you buy. If the staff object, go somewhere else to spend your money.*

5. *Turn your mattress once a week (unless not recommended by the manufacturer).*

6. *If you have severe back problems and your doctor recommends an orthopaedic bed, go to a medical supplier. (See list at back of book). Beware of advertisements offering orthopaedic beds.*

7. *If you suffer from swollen ankles, raise the bottom of your bed so that your feet are higher than your body. This can help to bring down the swelling. Wooden blocks are ideal.*

8. *Spend as much as you can afford on pillows. Again cheap ones do not pay in the long run. A good buy is duck down and feather. The best are Siberian Goose down and Hungarian Goose down. Also "V" shaped neck cushions can be most comfortable. Larger back versions are also available. Don't forget to have your pillows and duvets cleaned at regular intervals.*

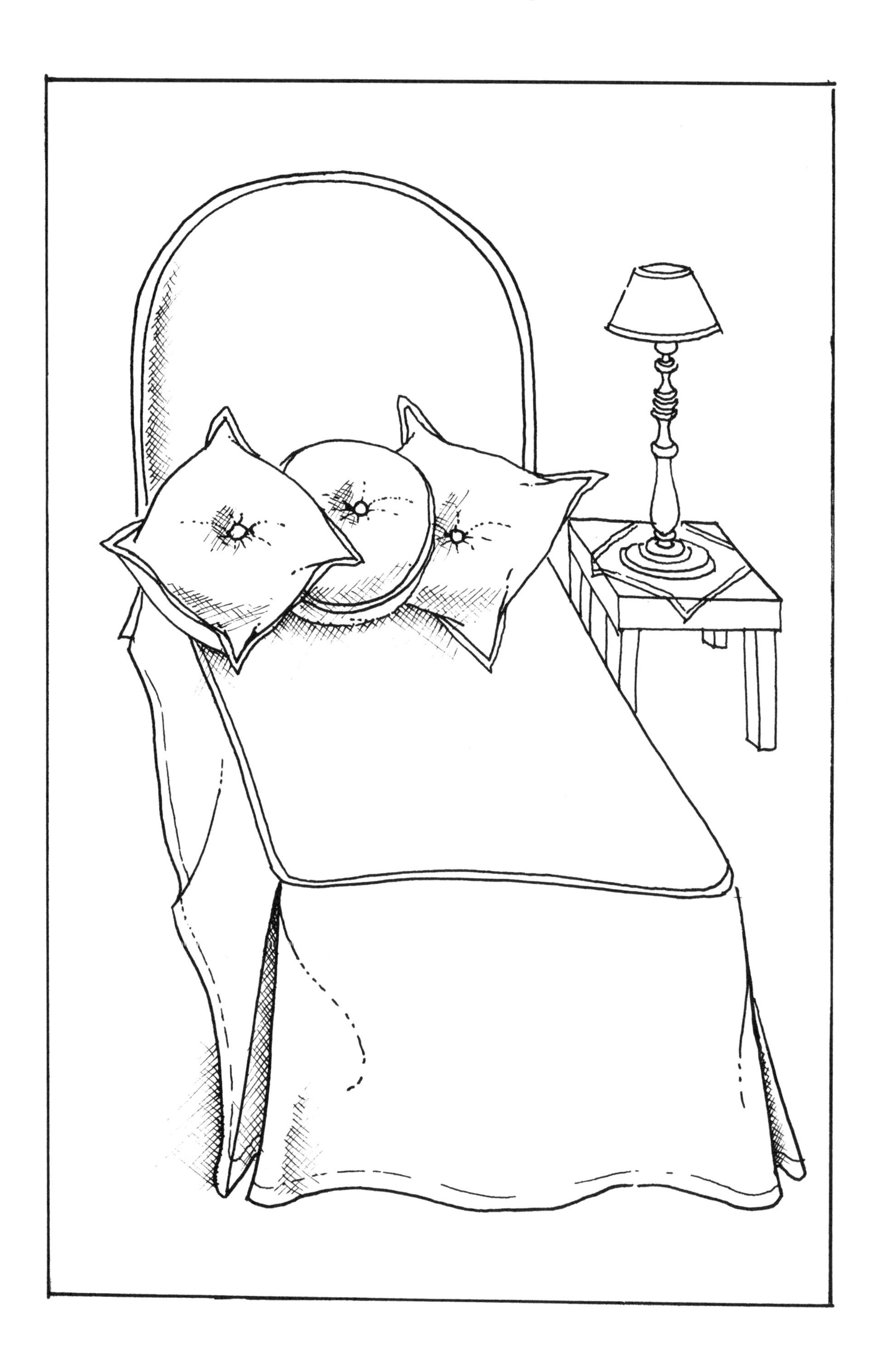

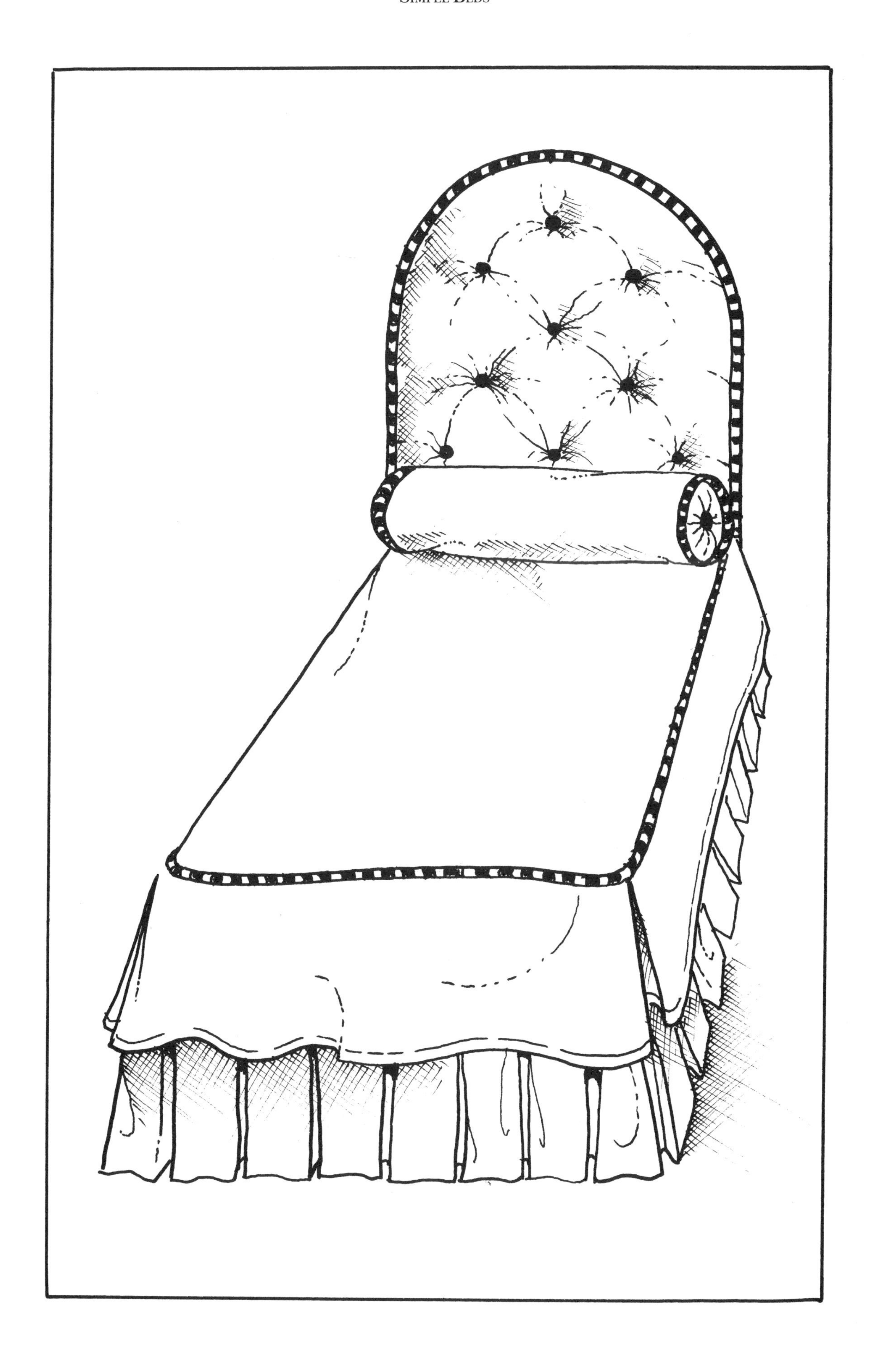

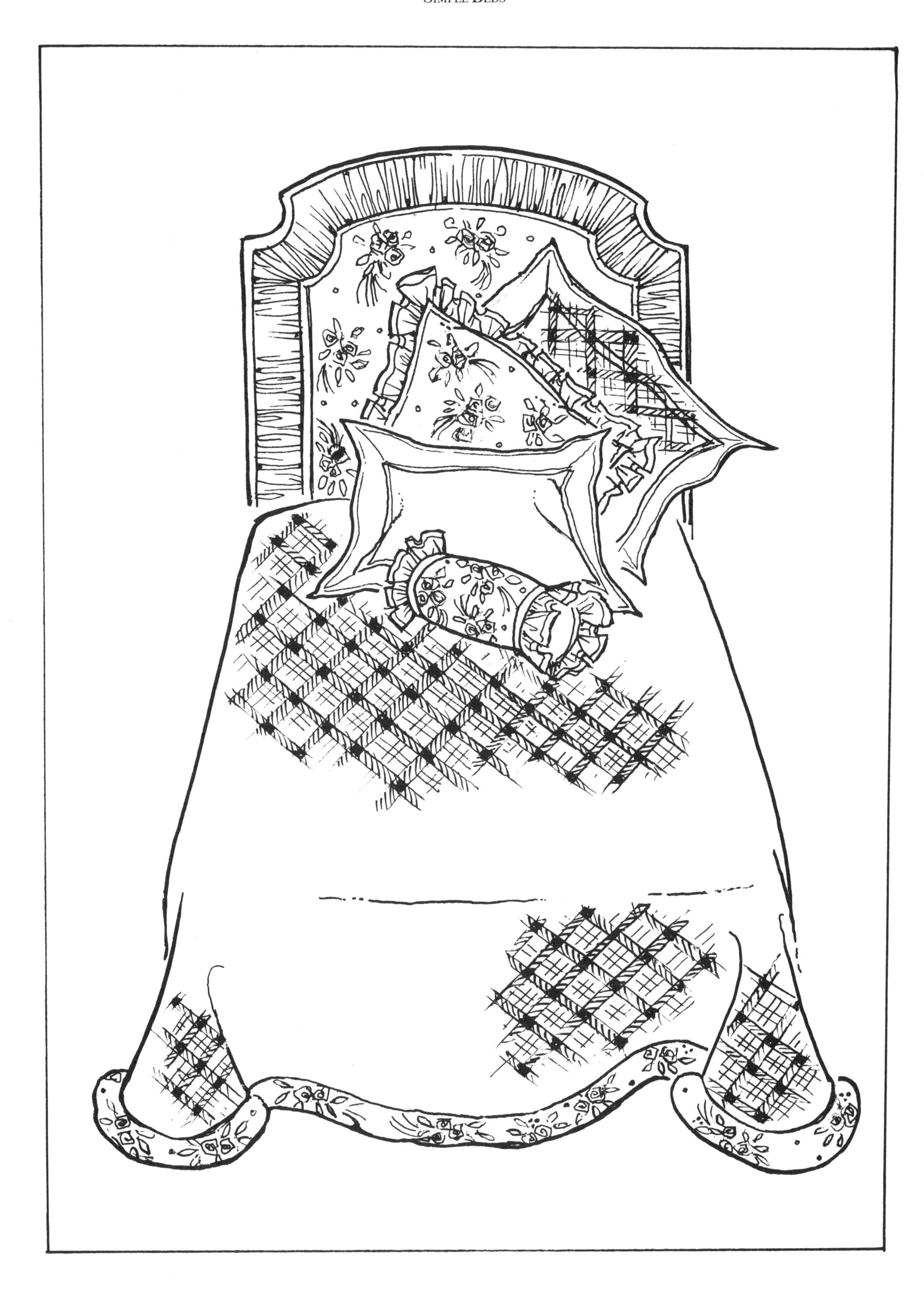

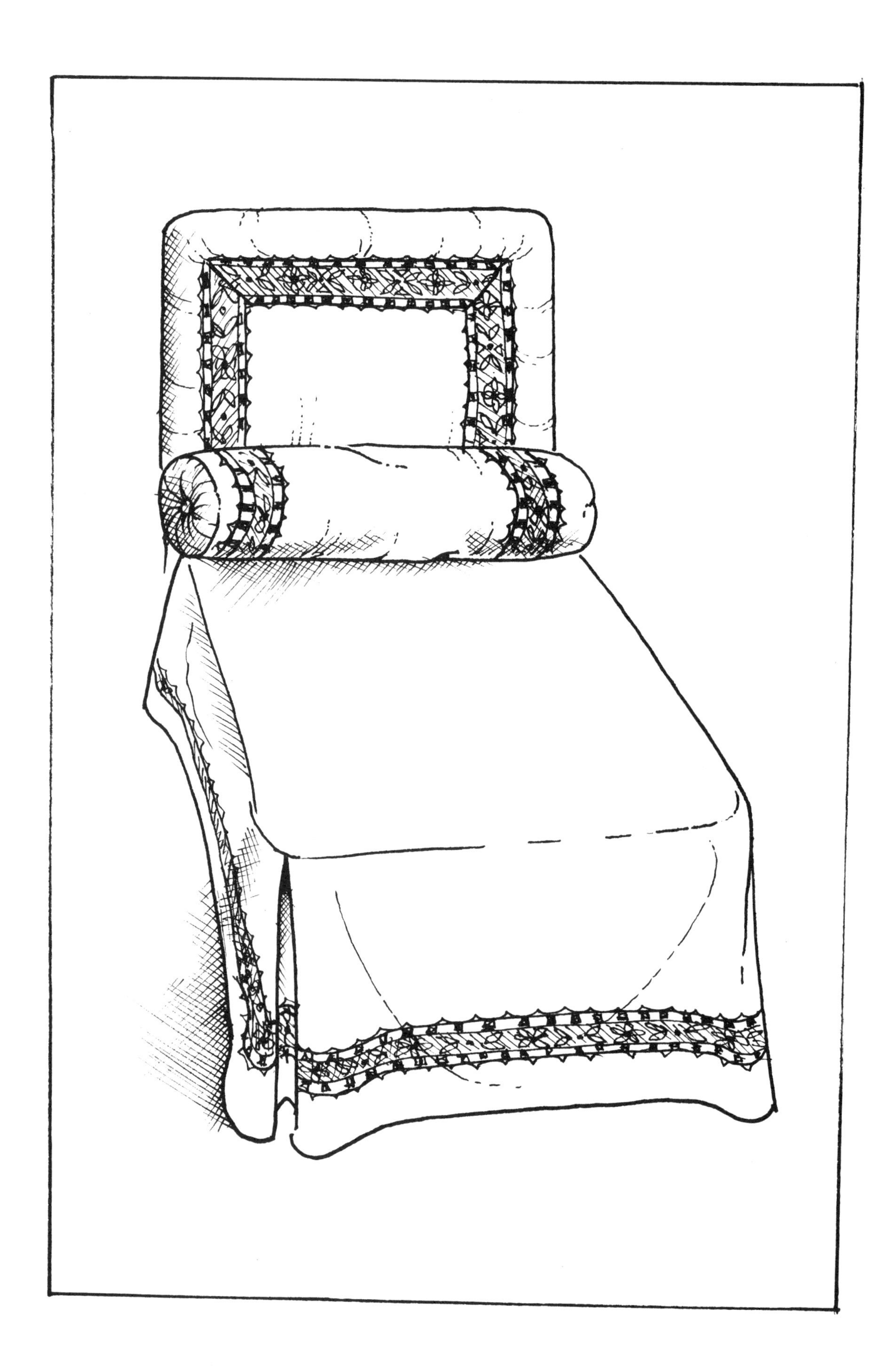

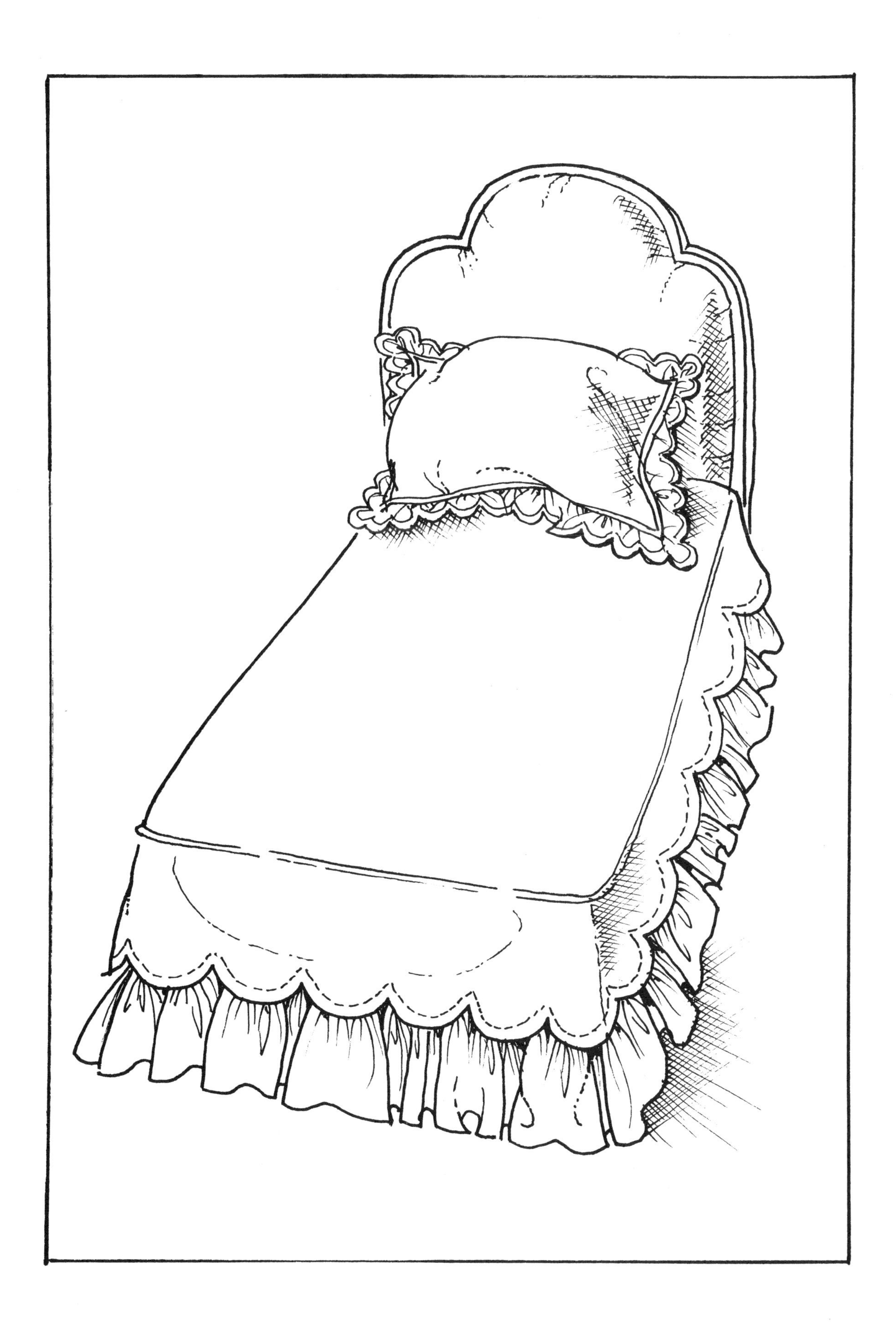

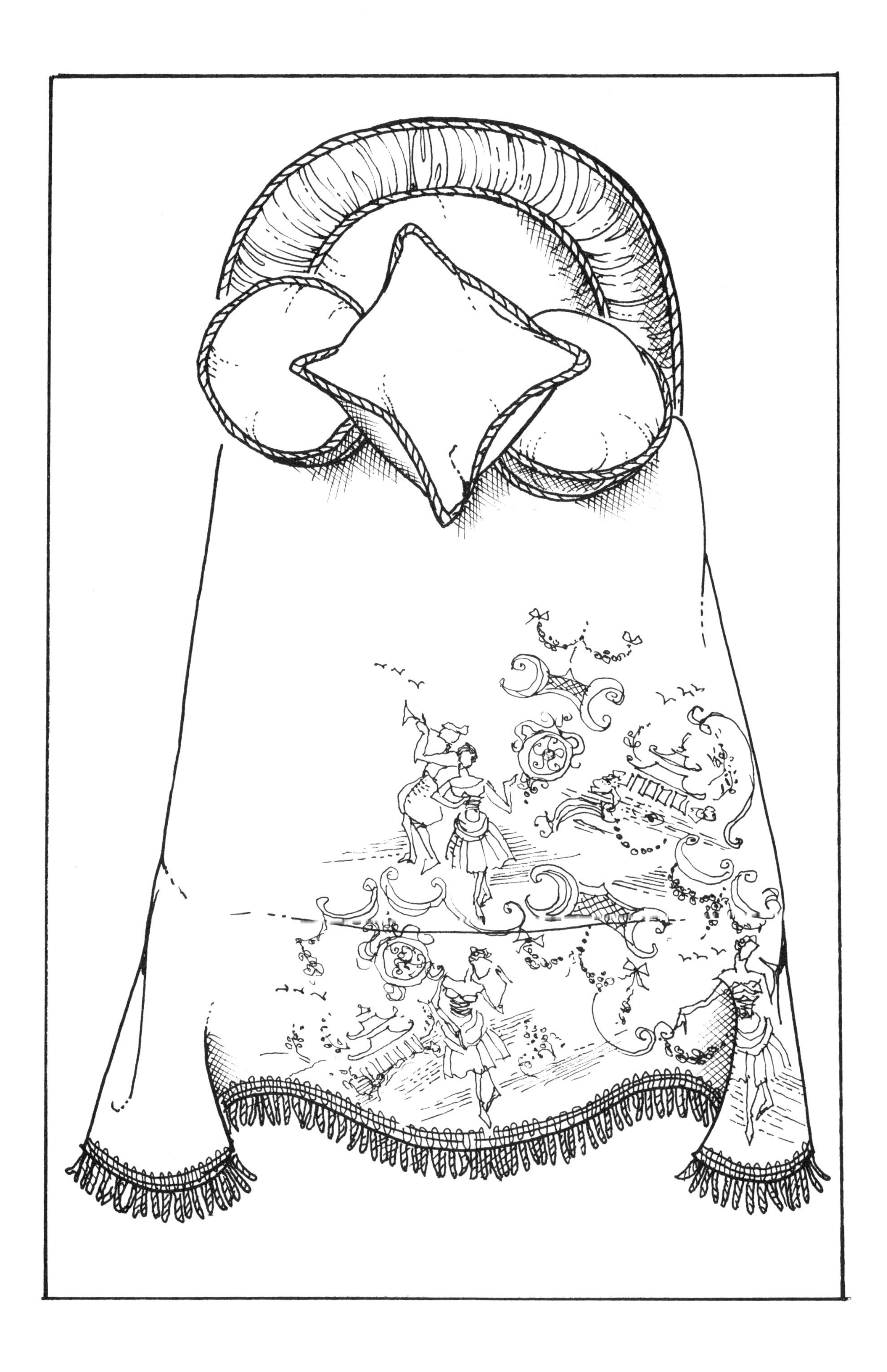

Four Poster

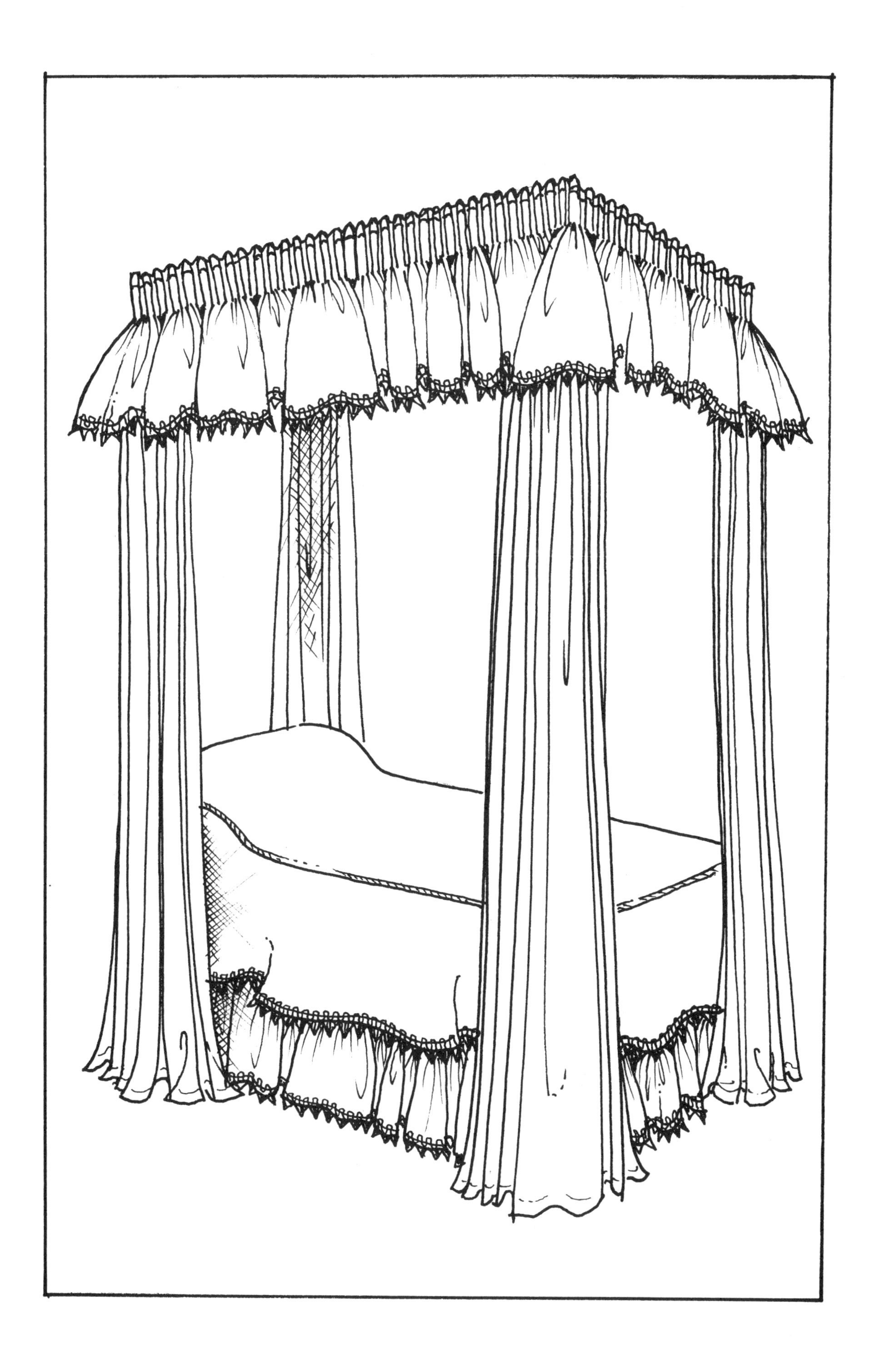

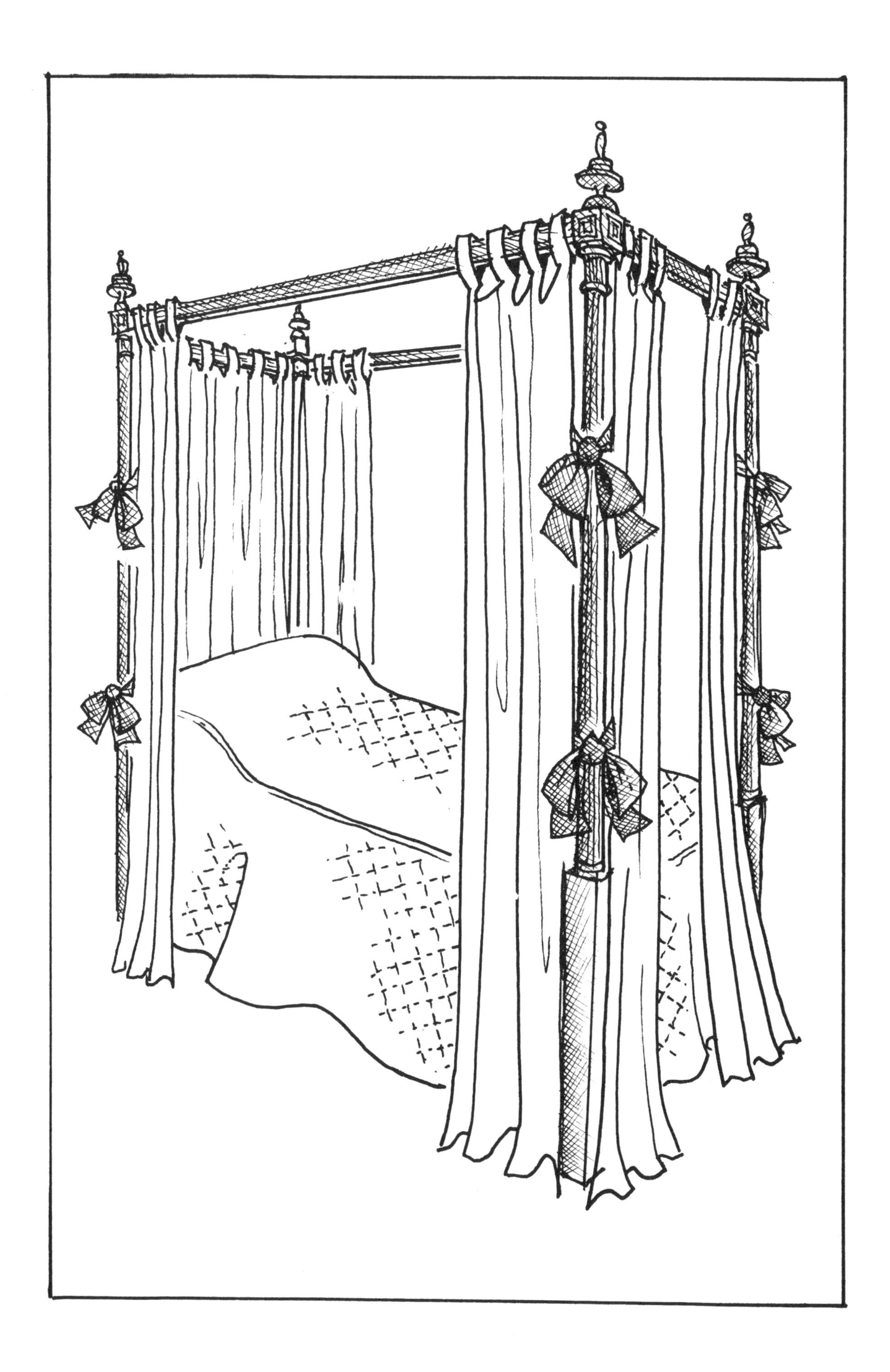

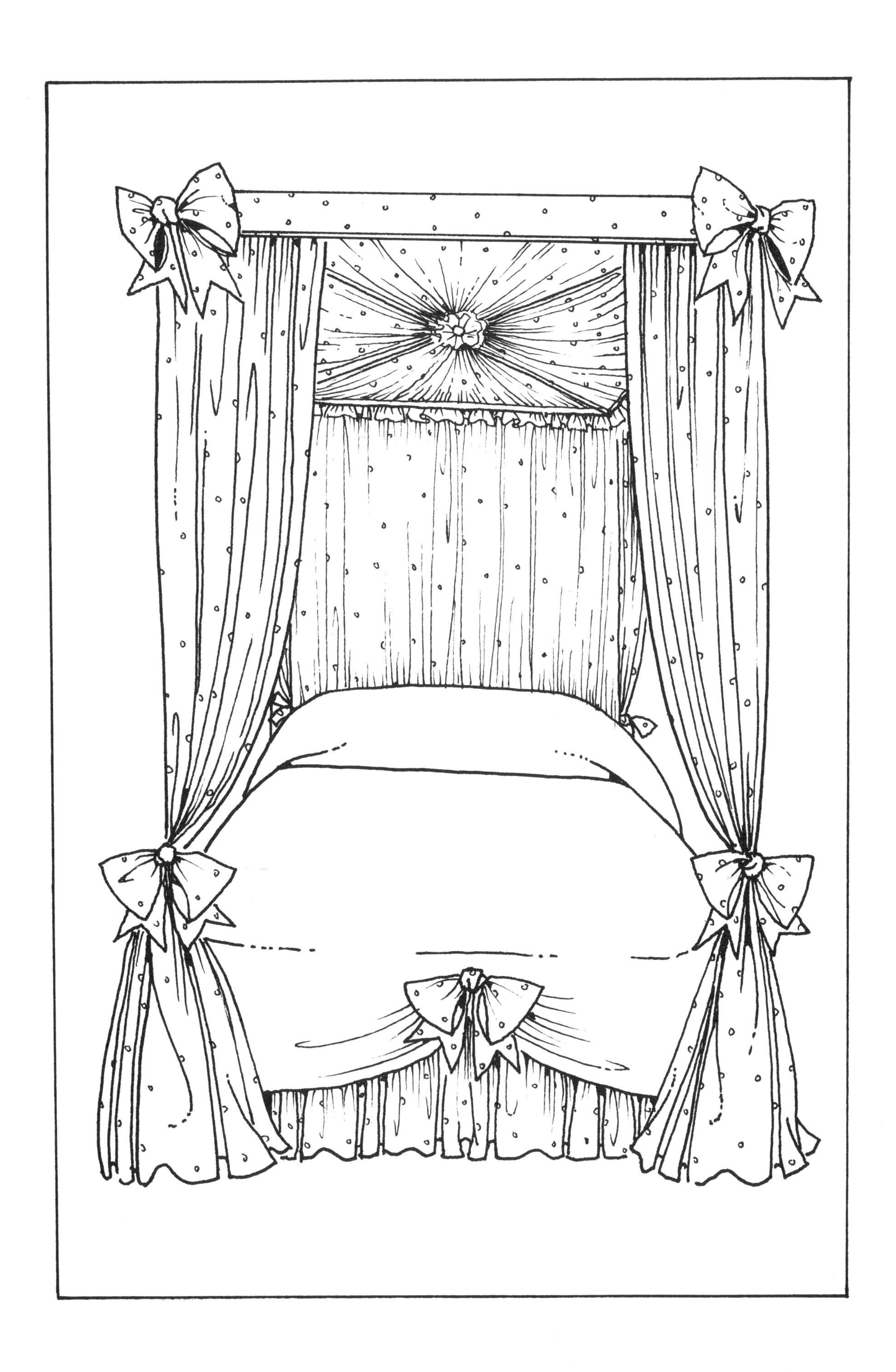

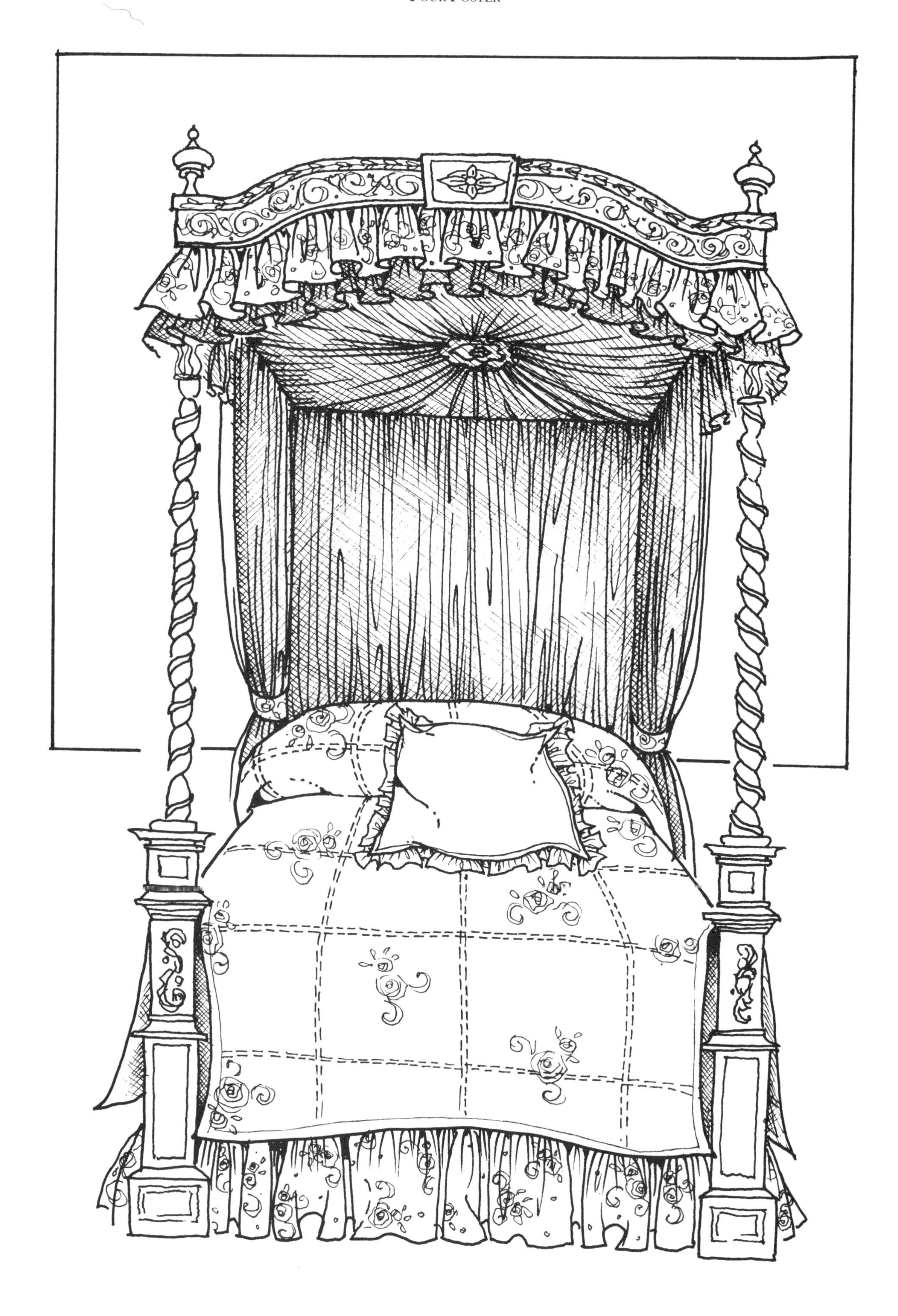

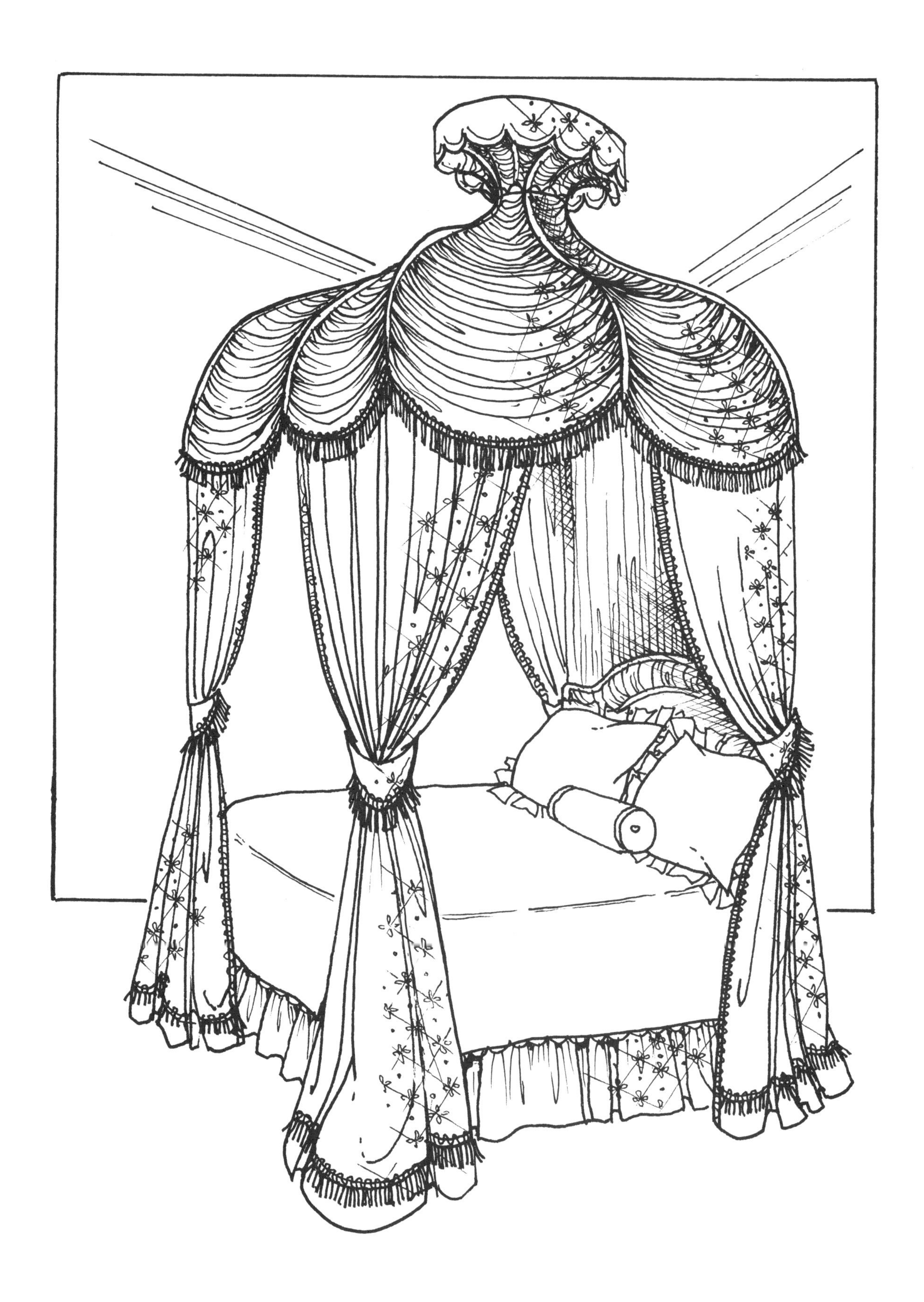

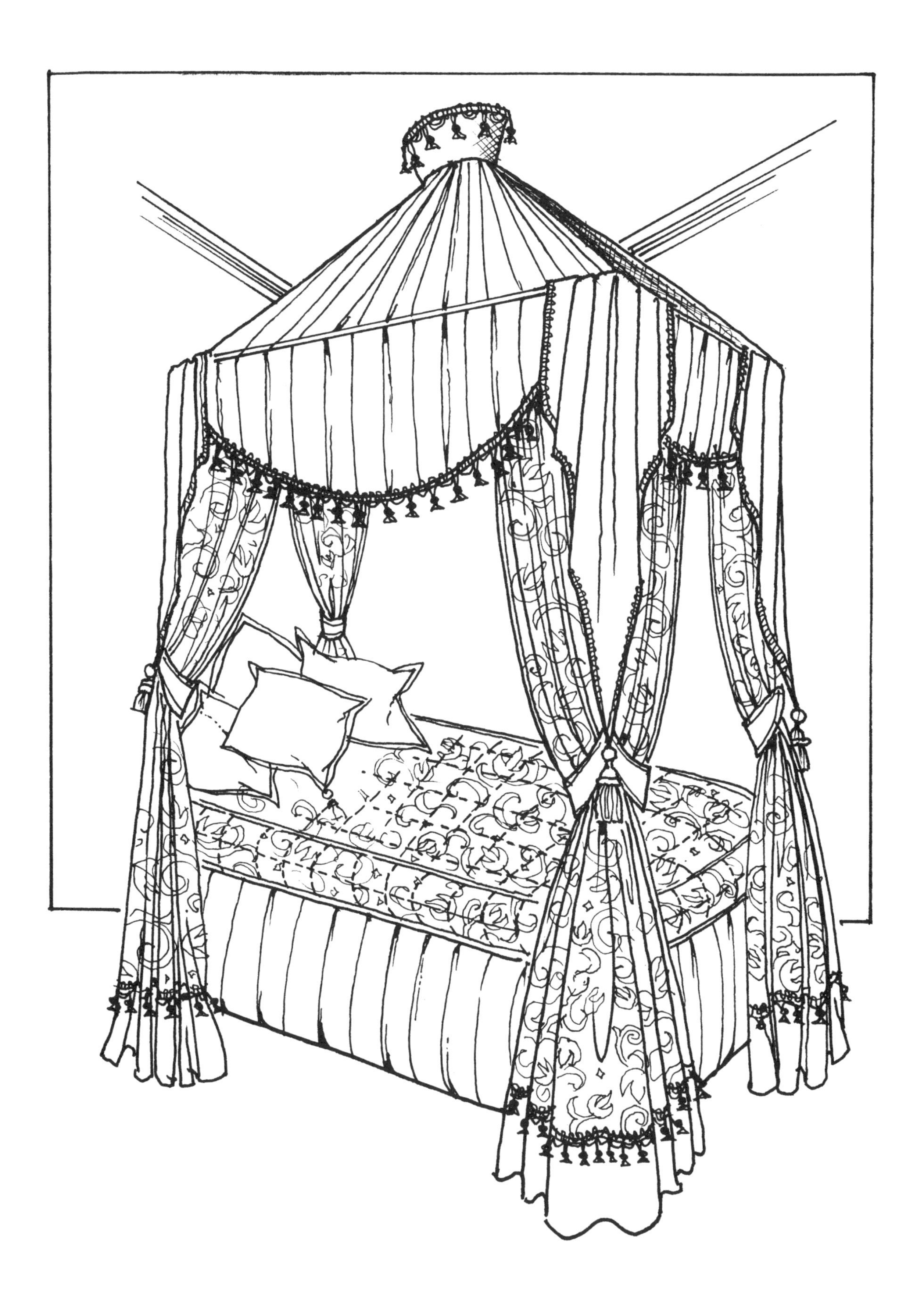

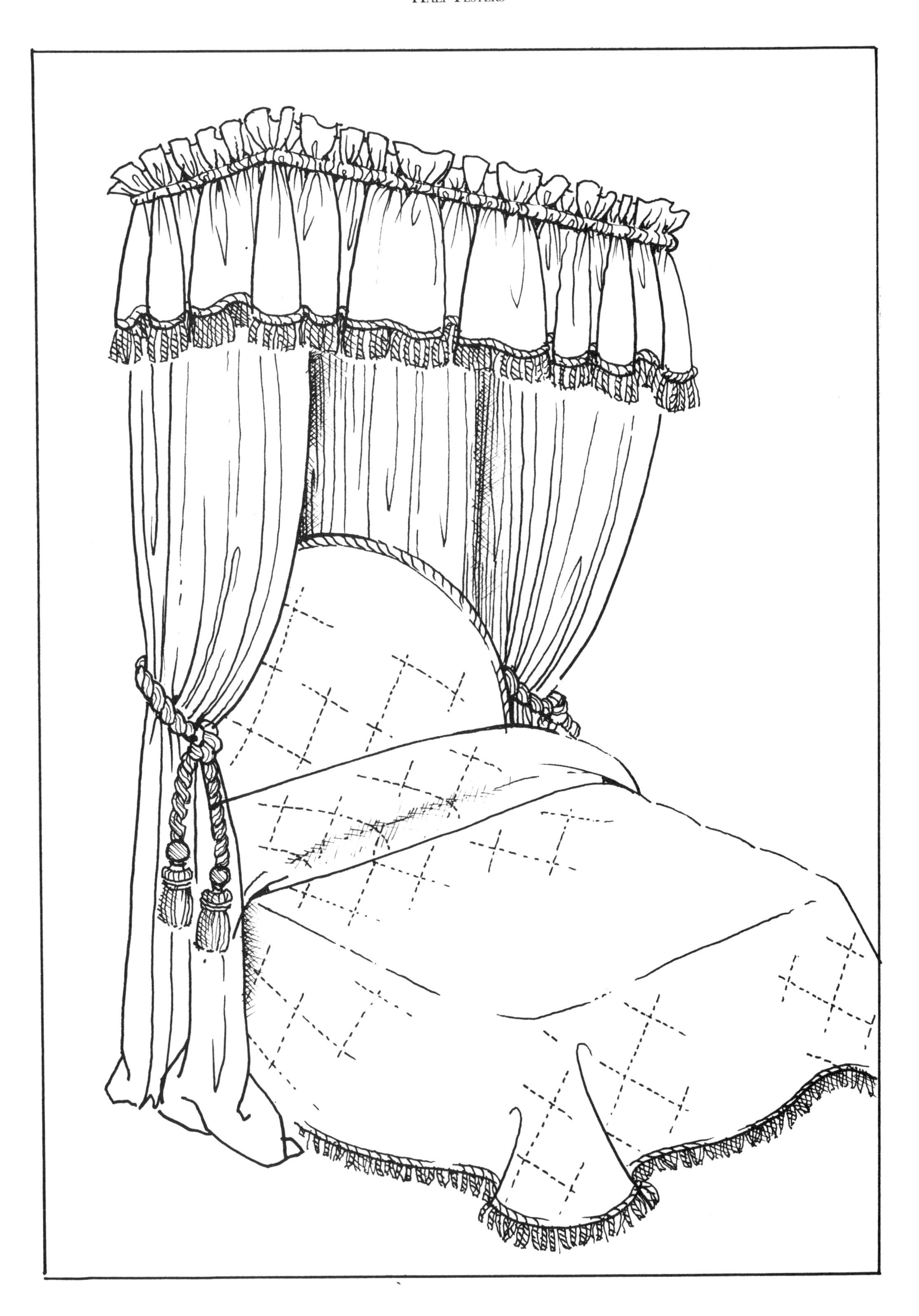

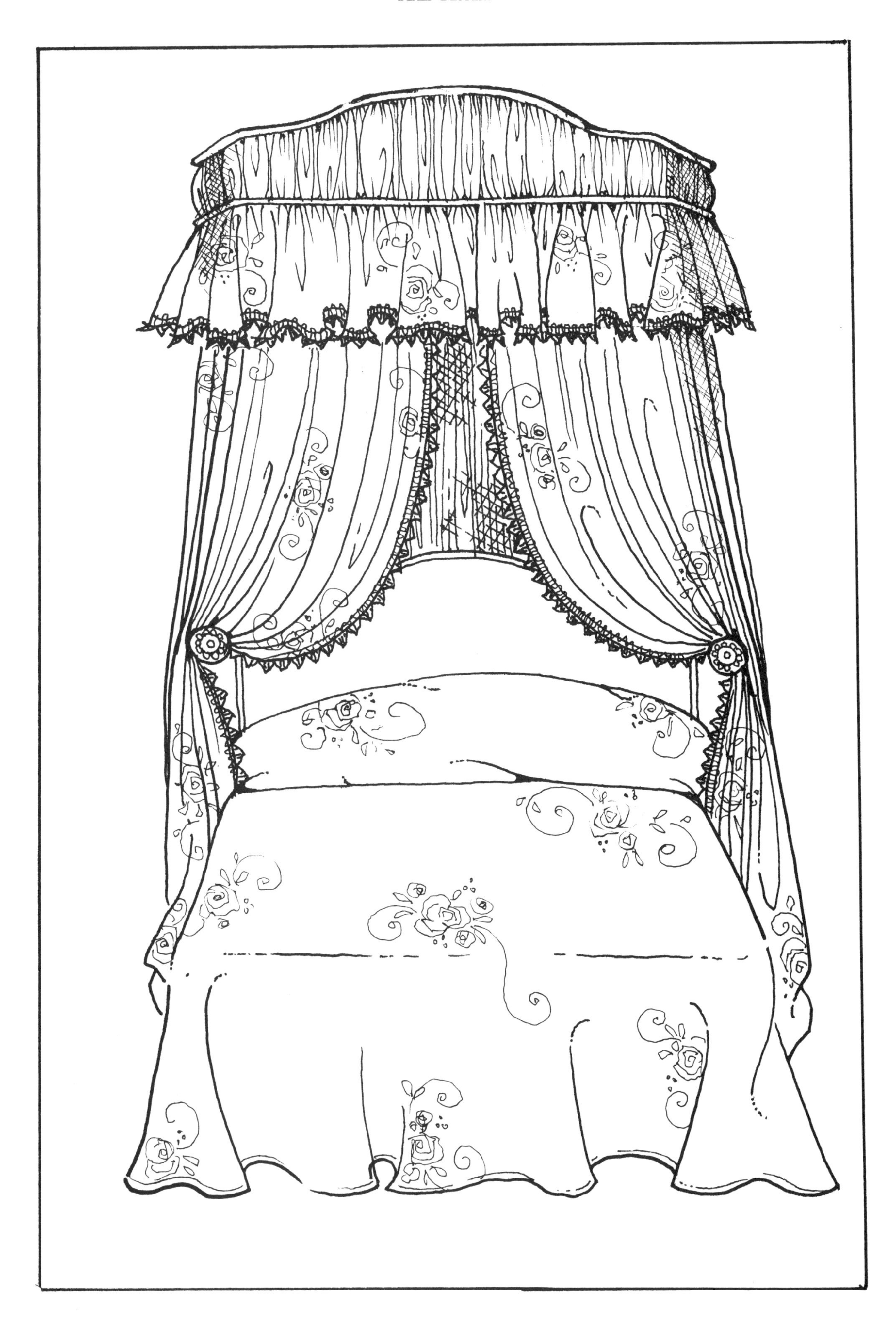

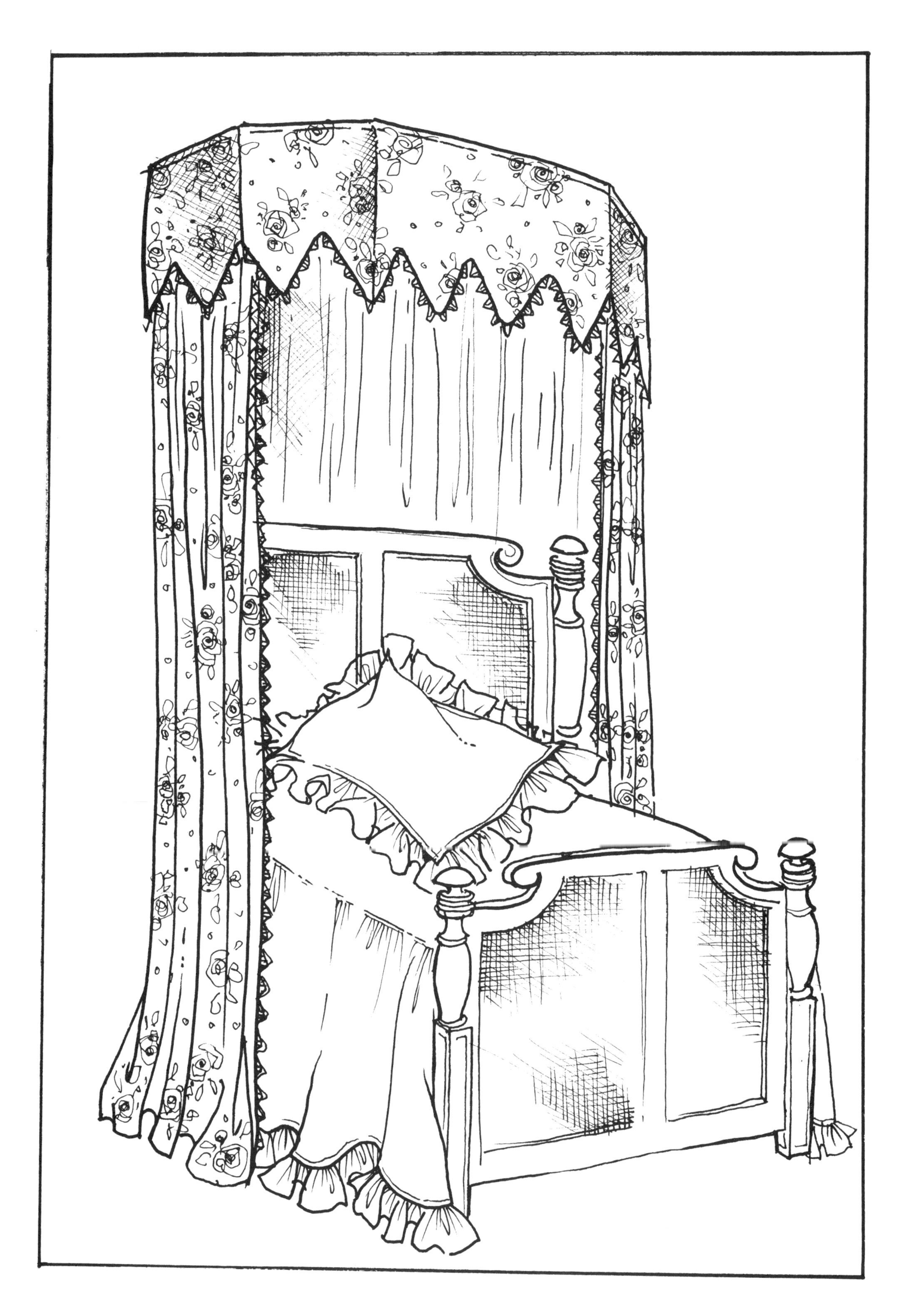

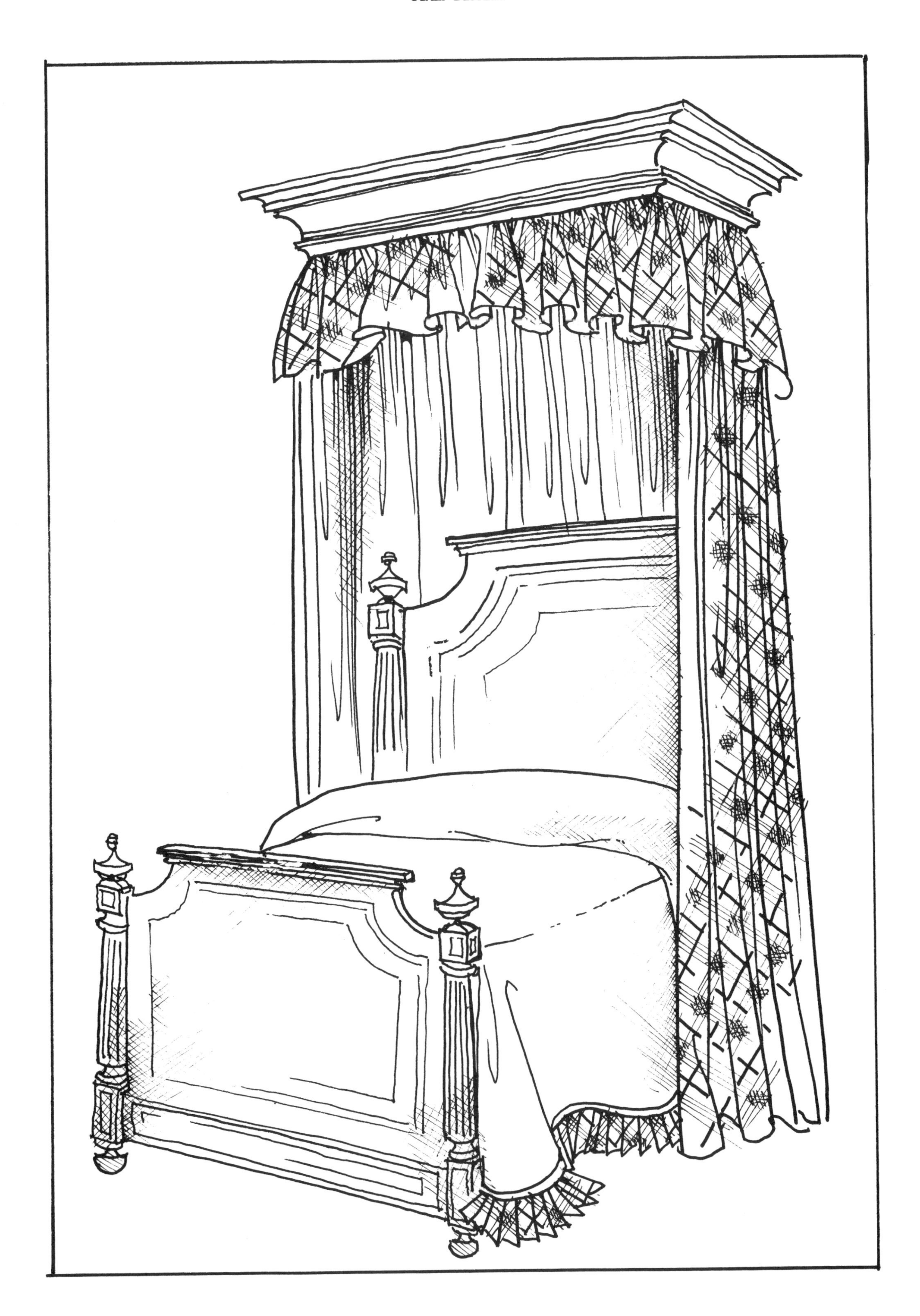

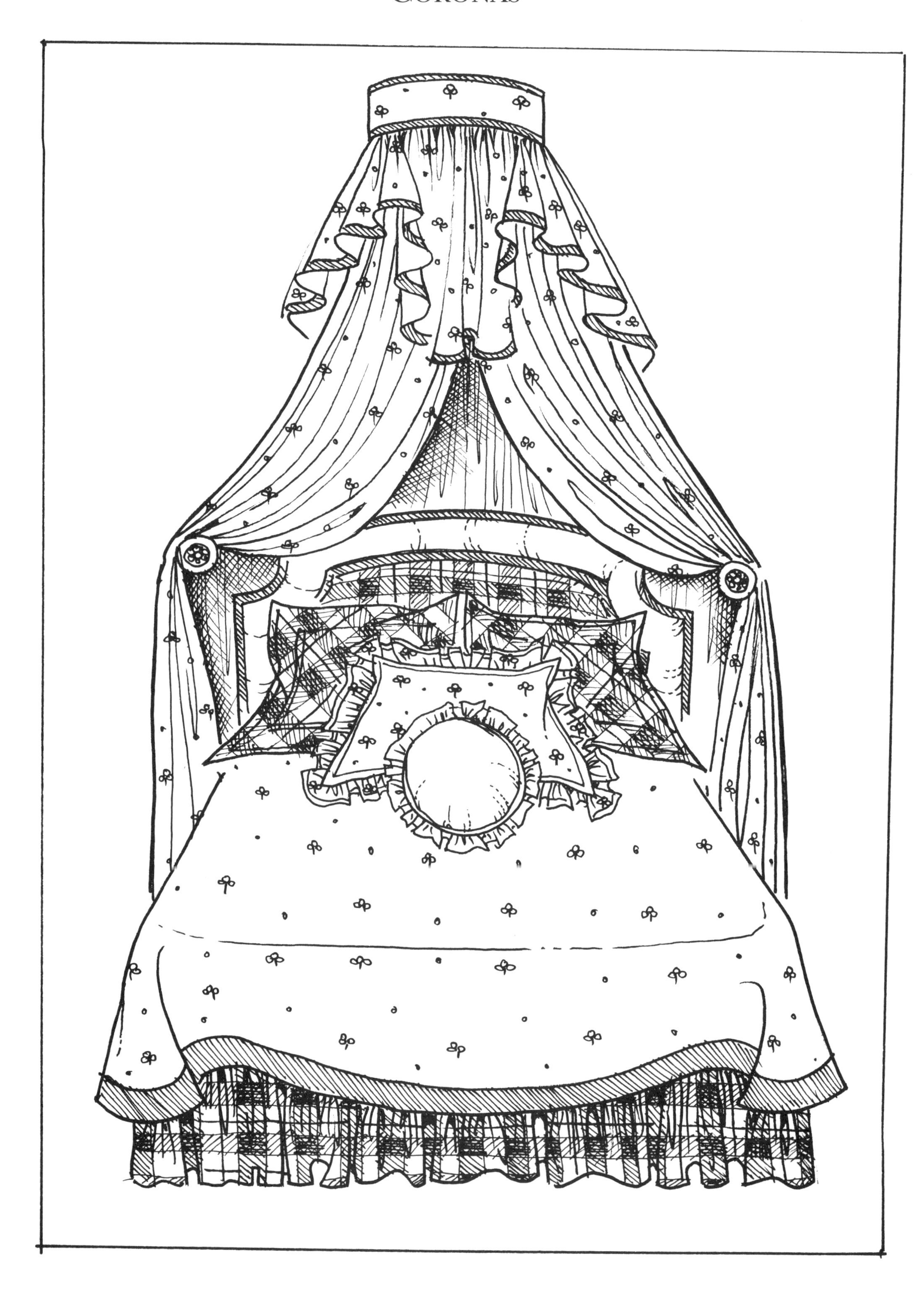

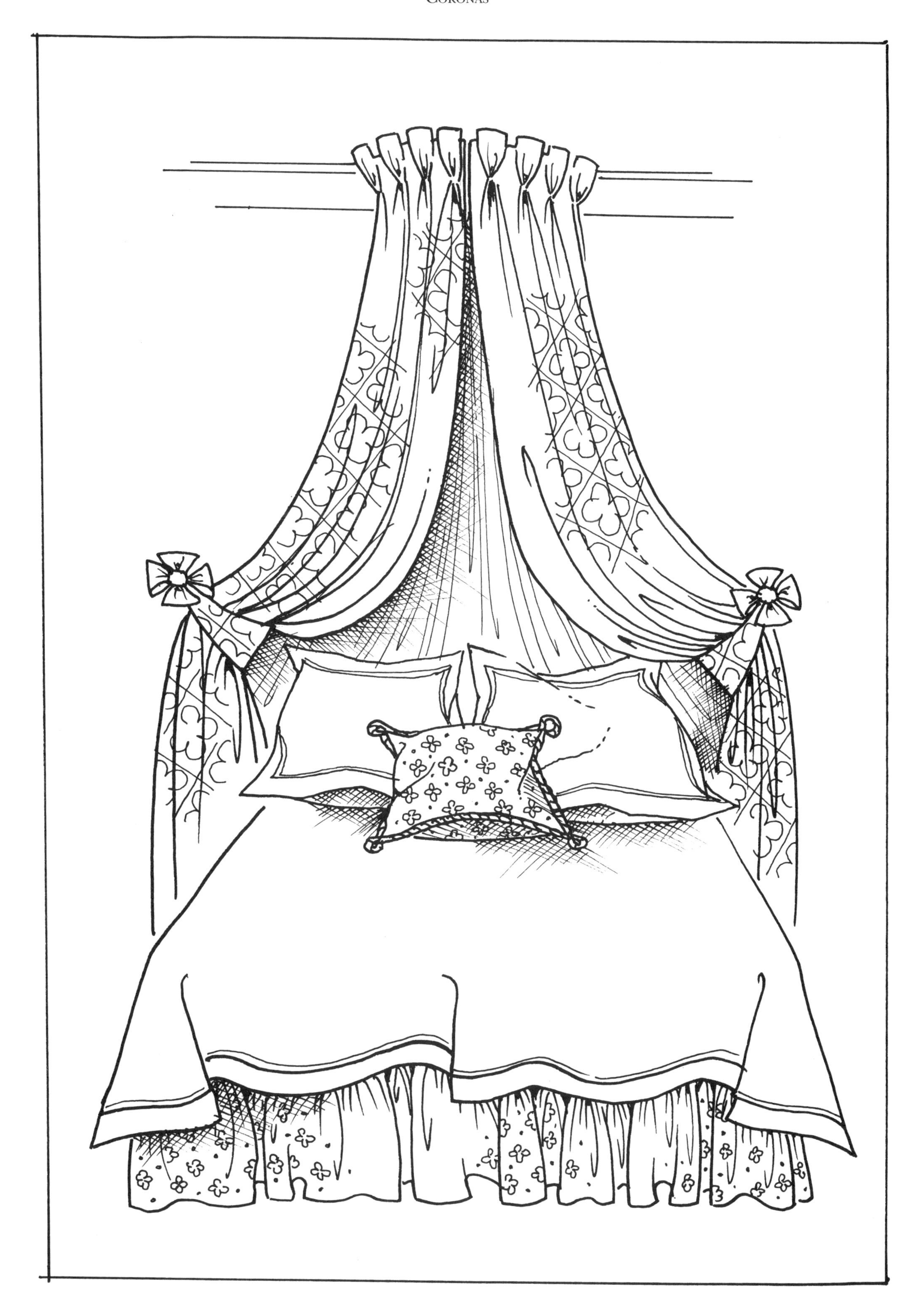

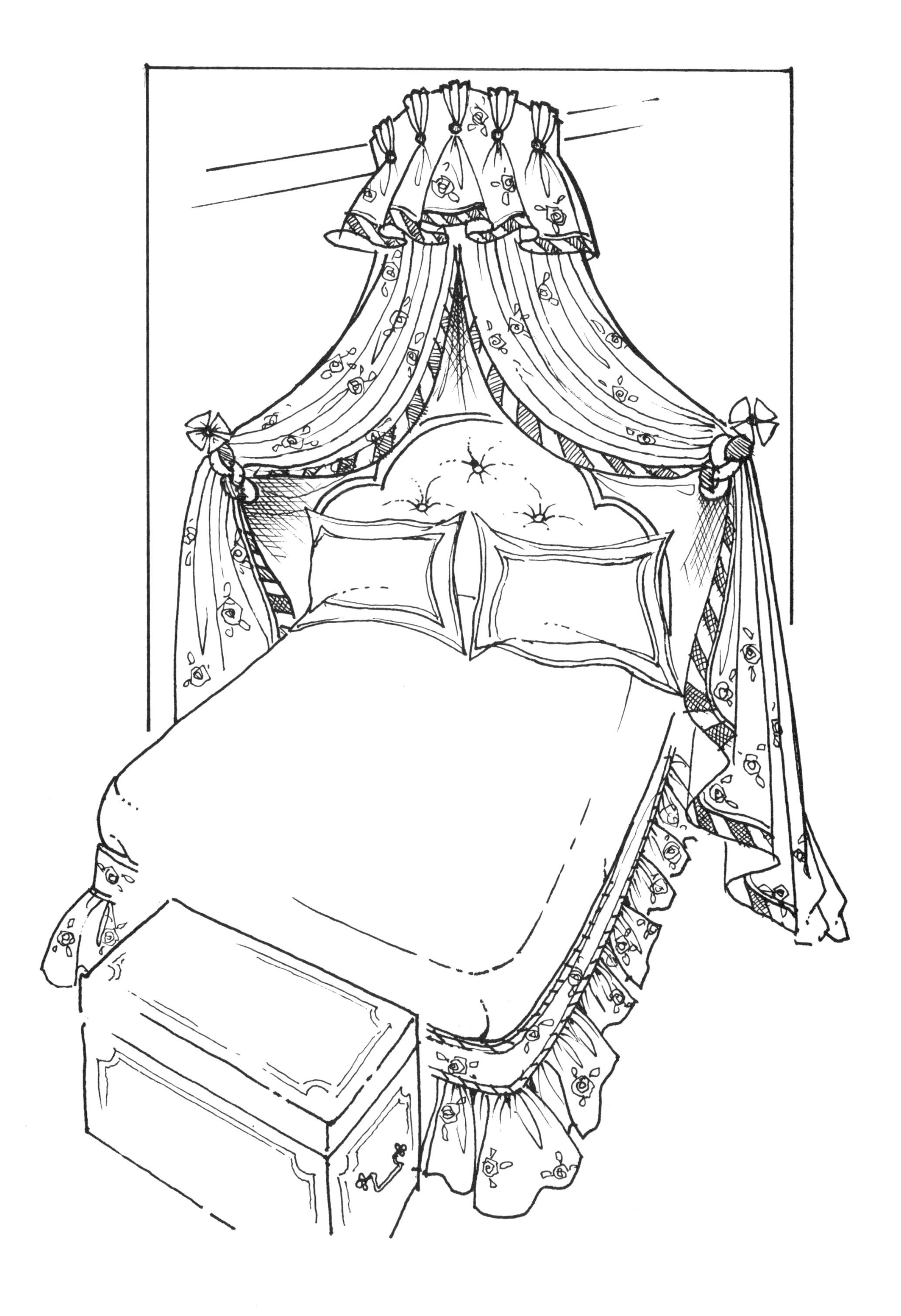

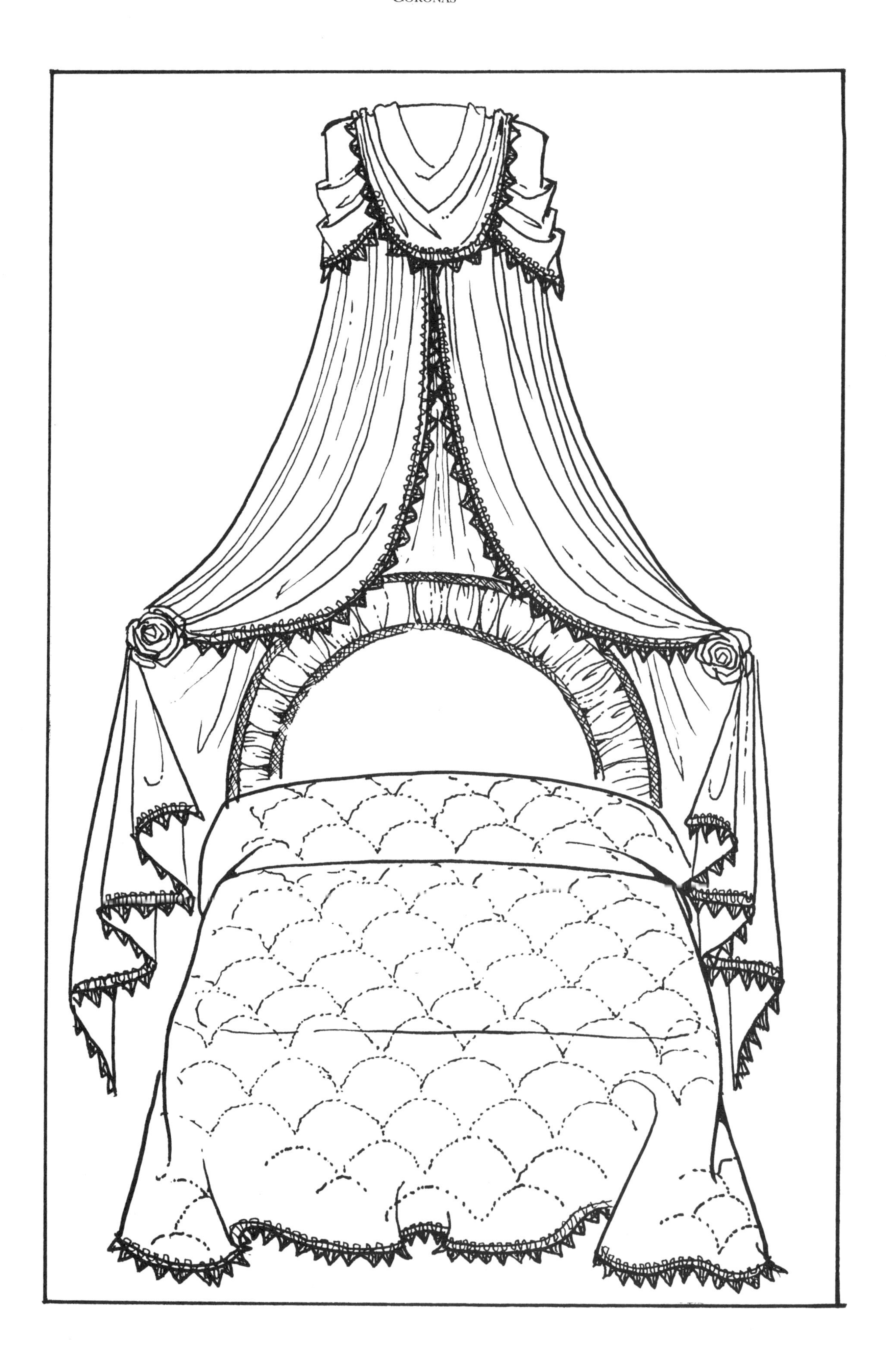

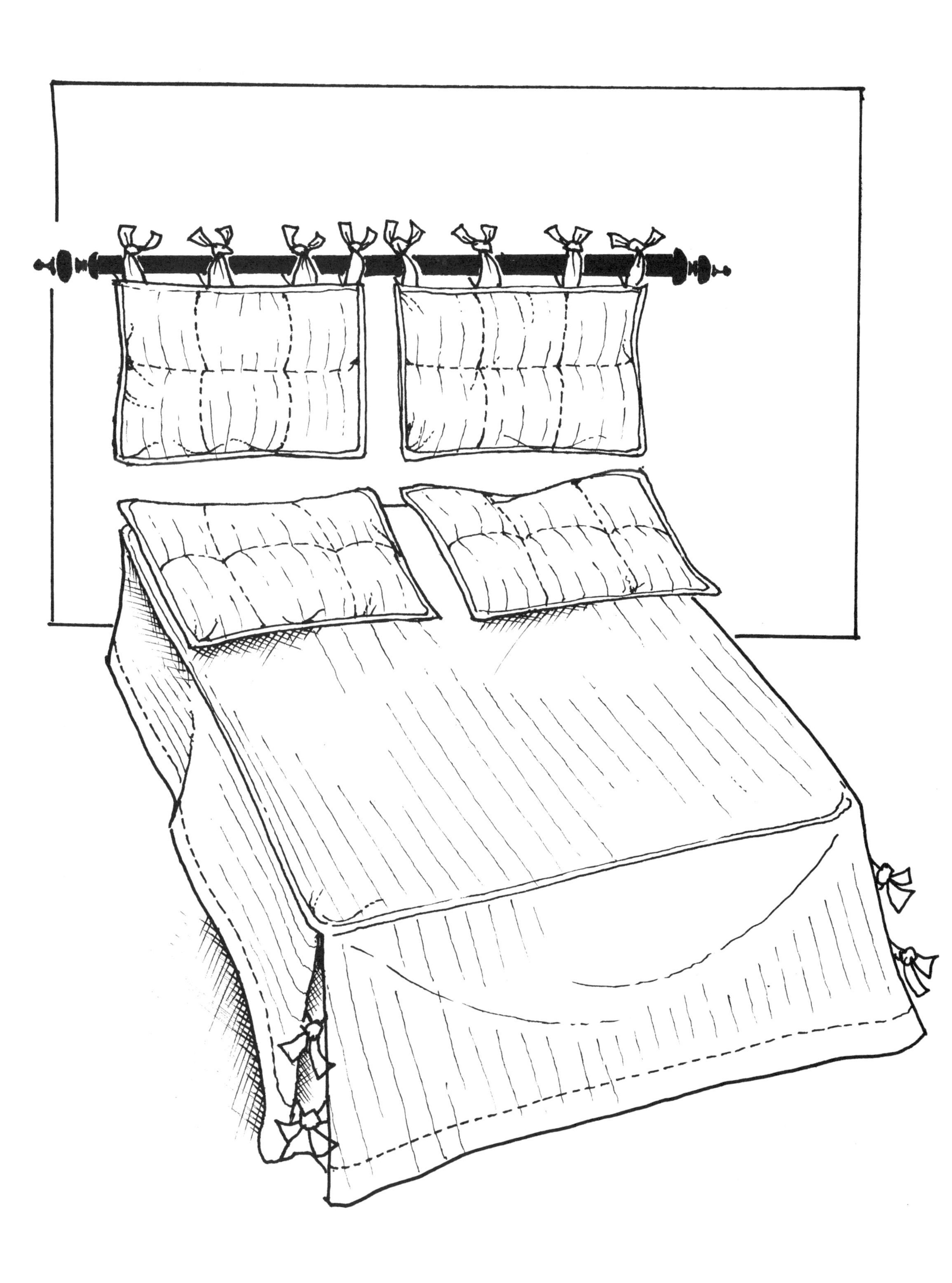

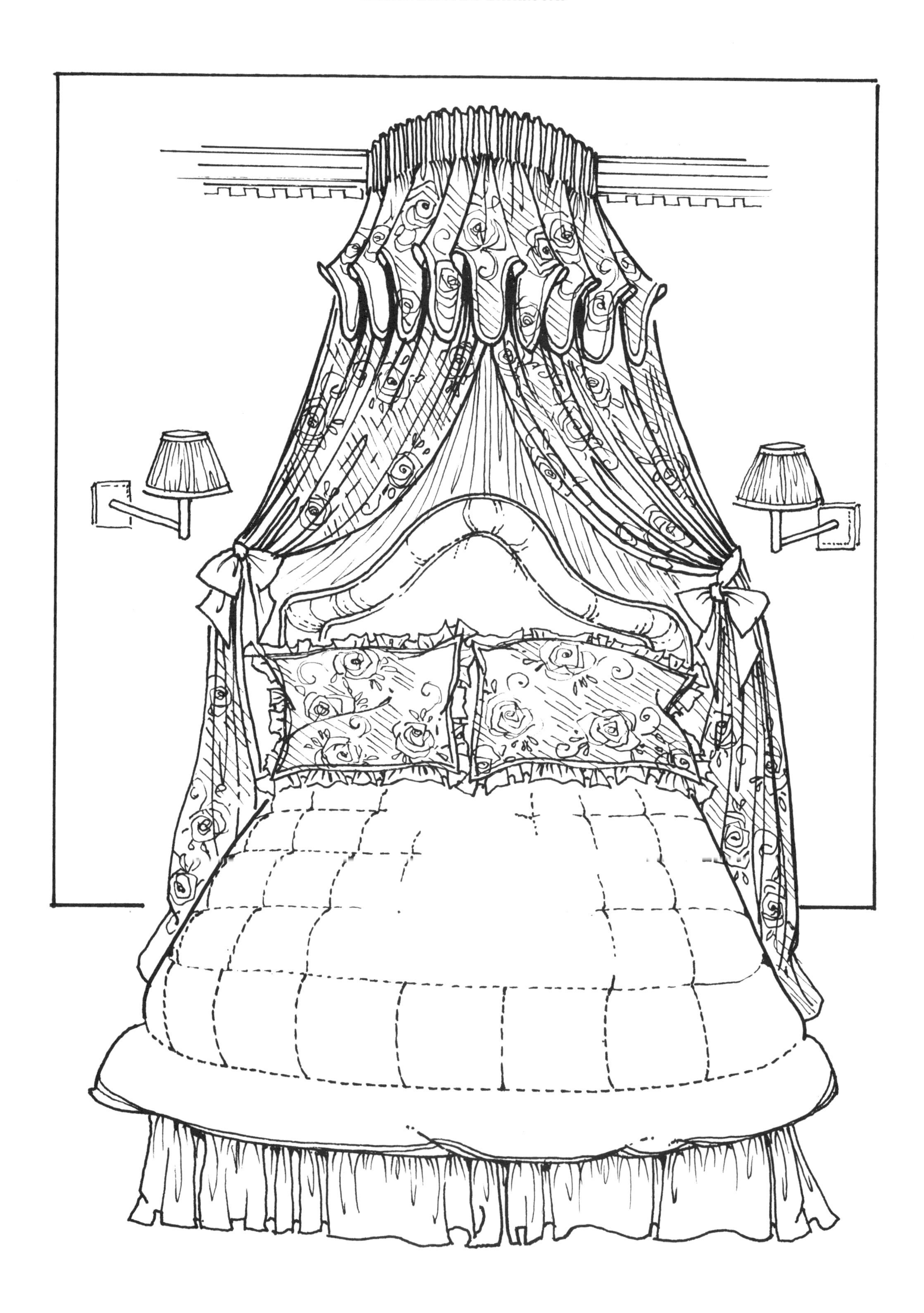

Welcome

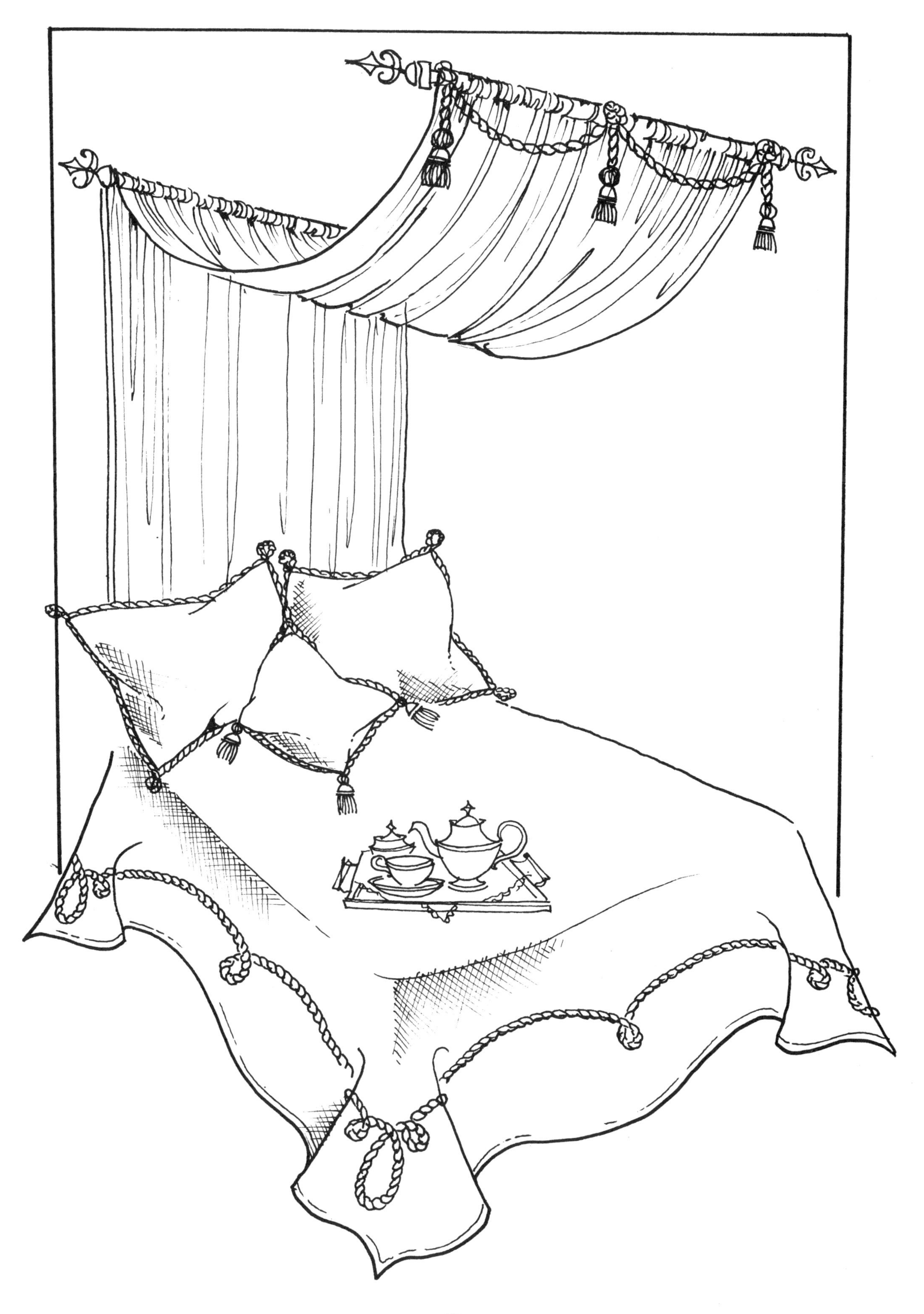

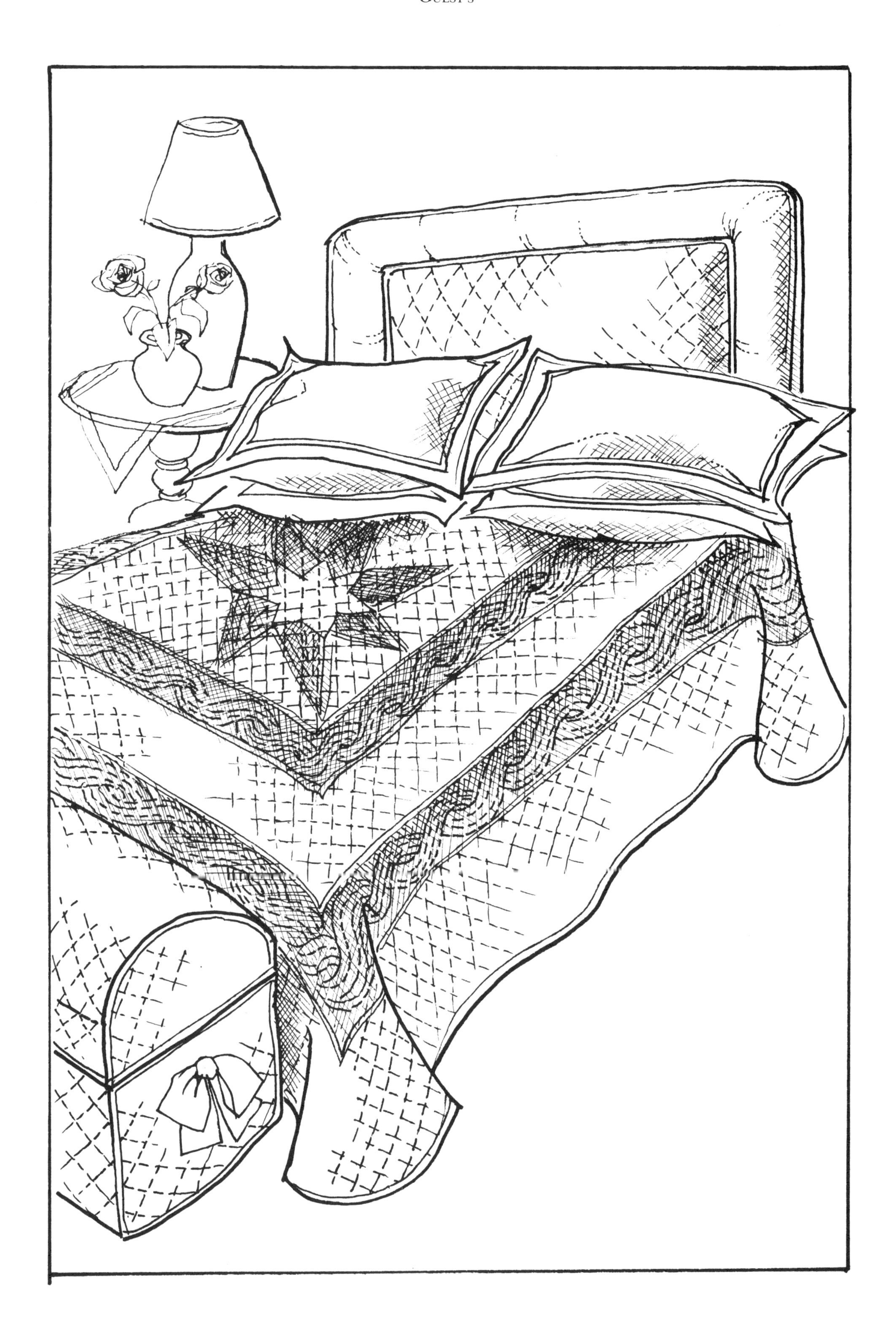

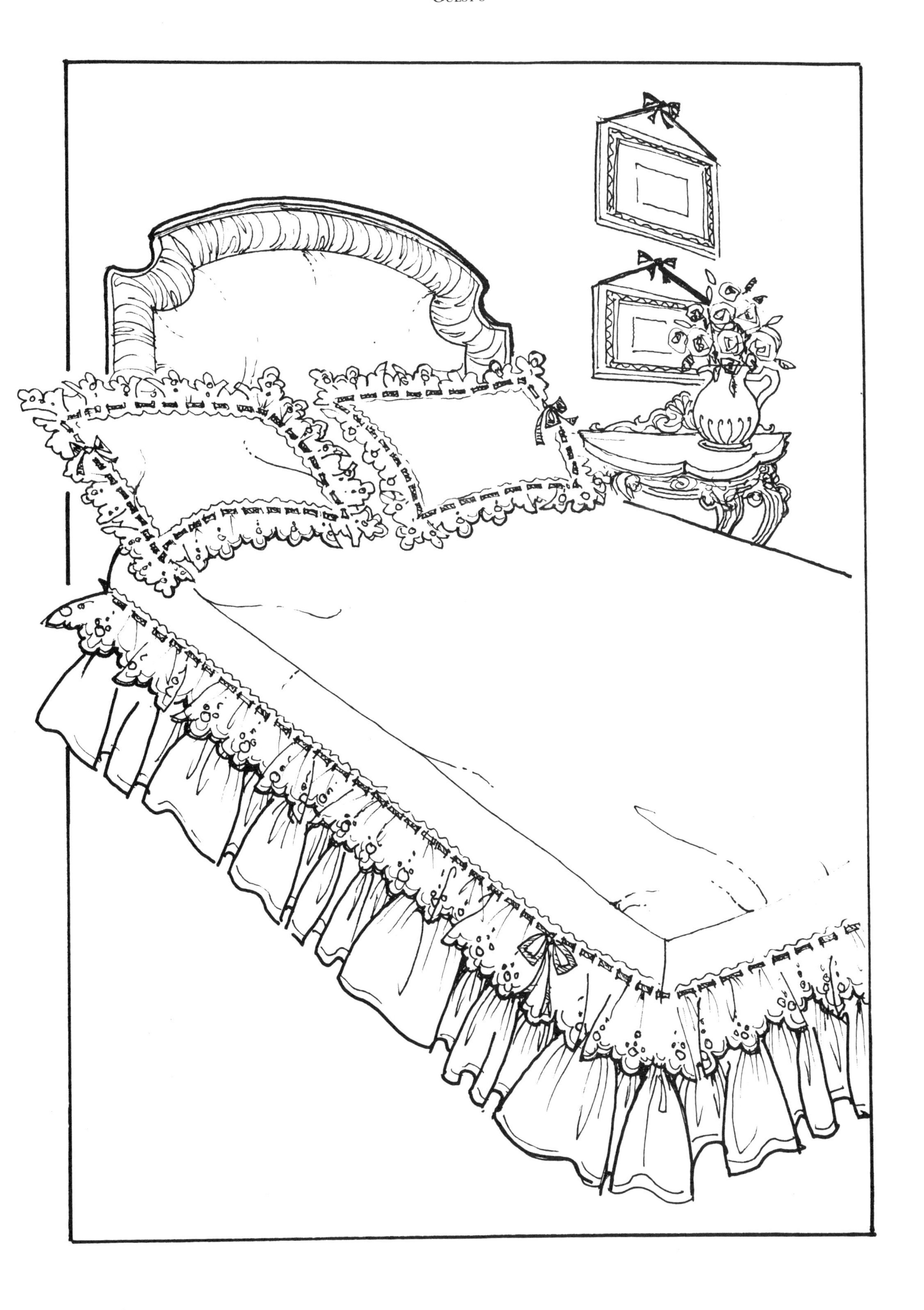

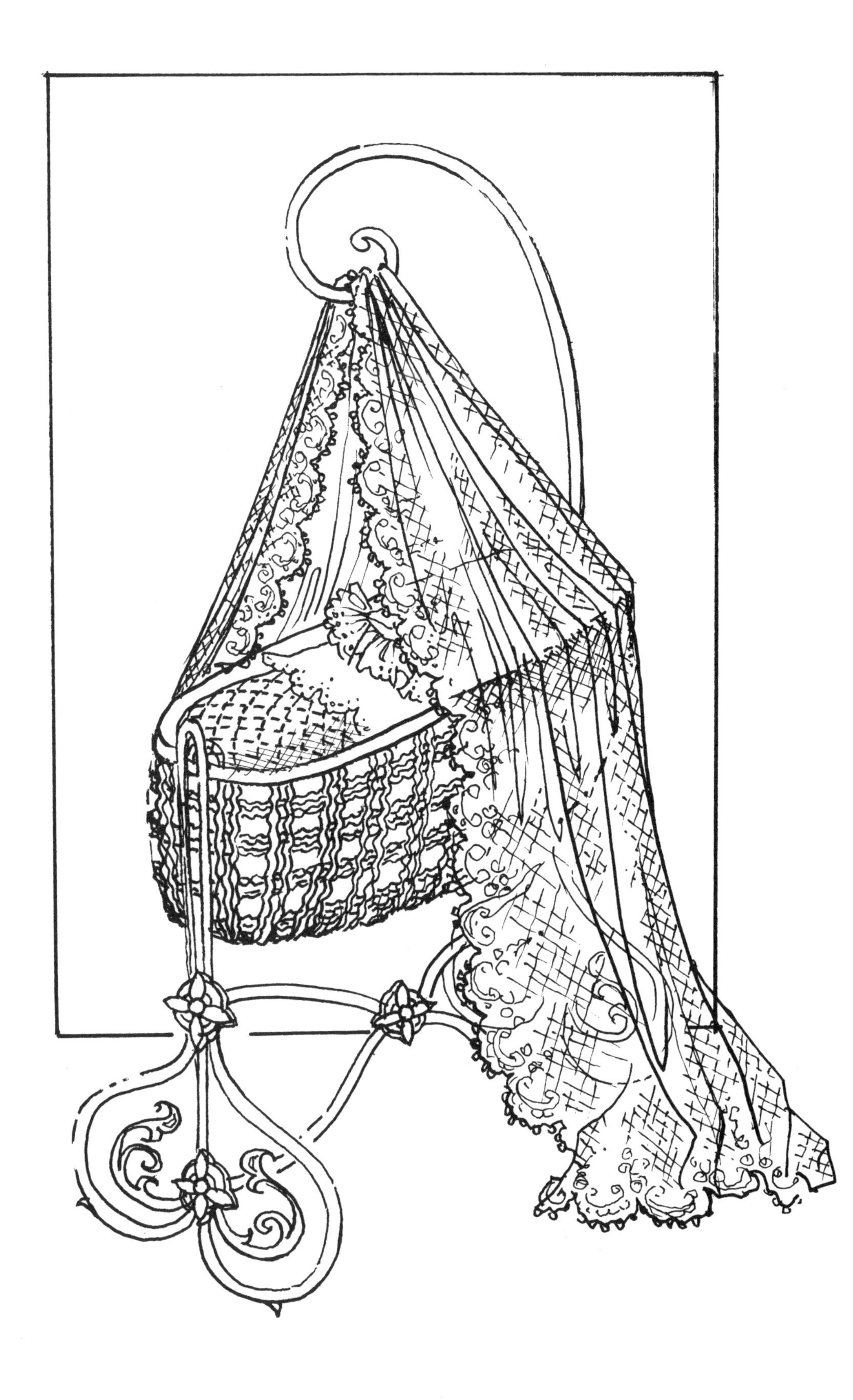

5

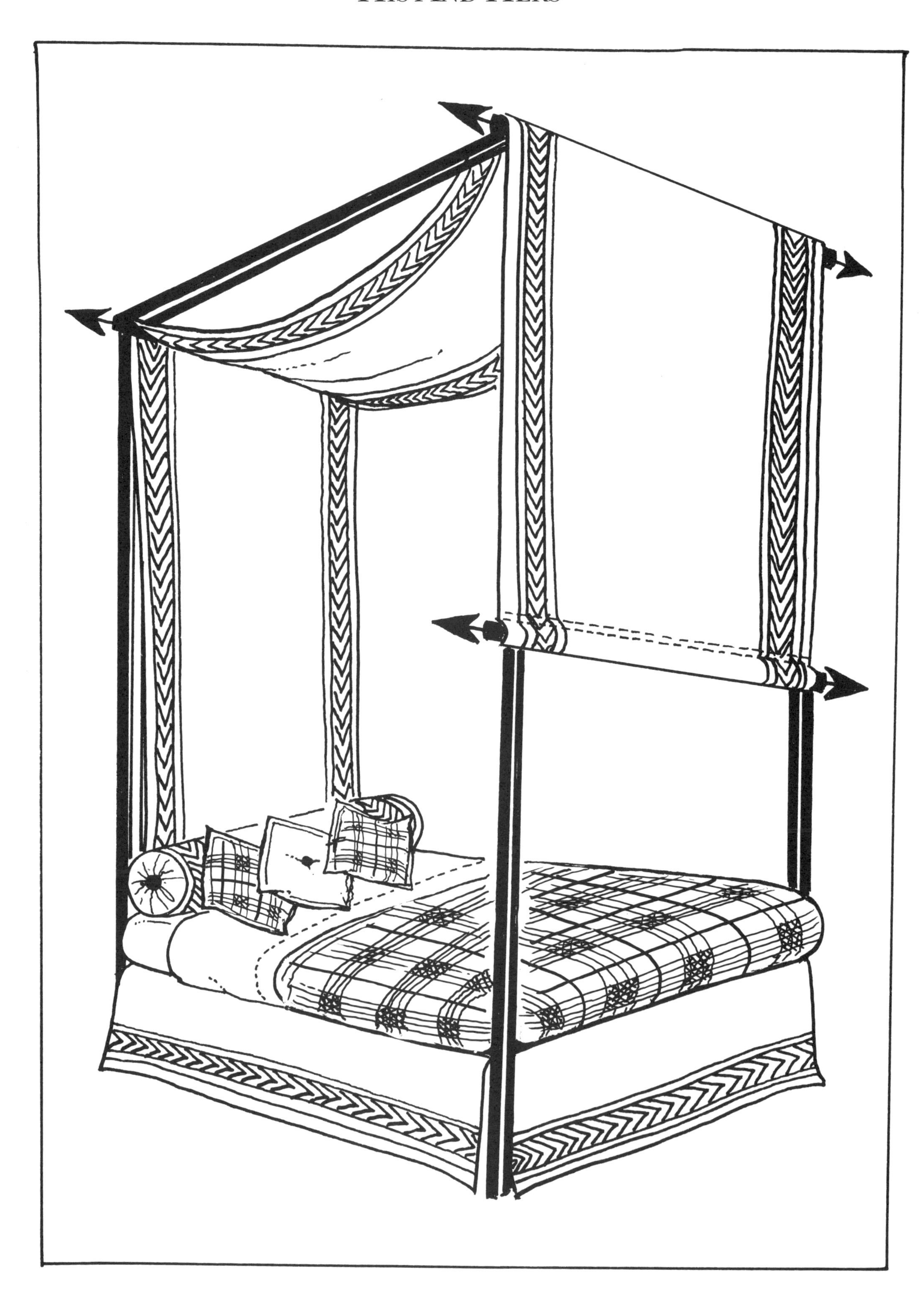

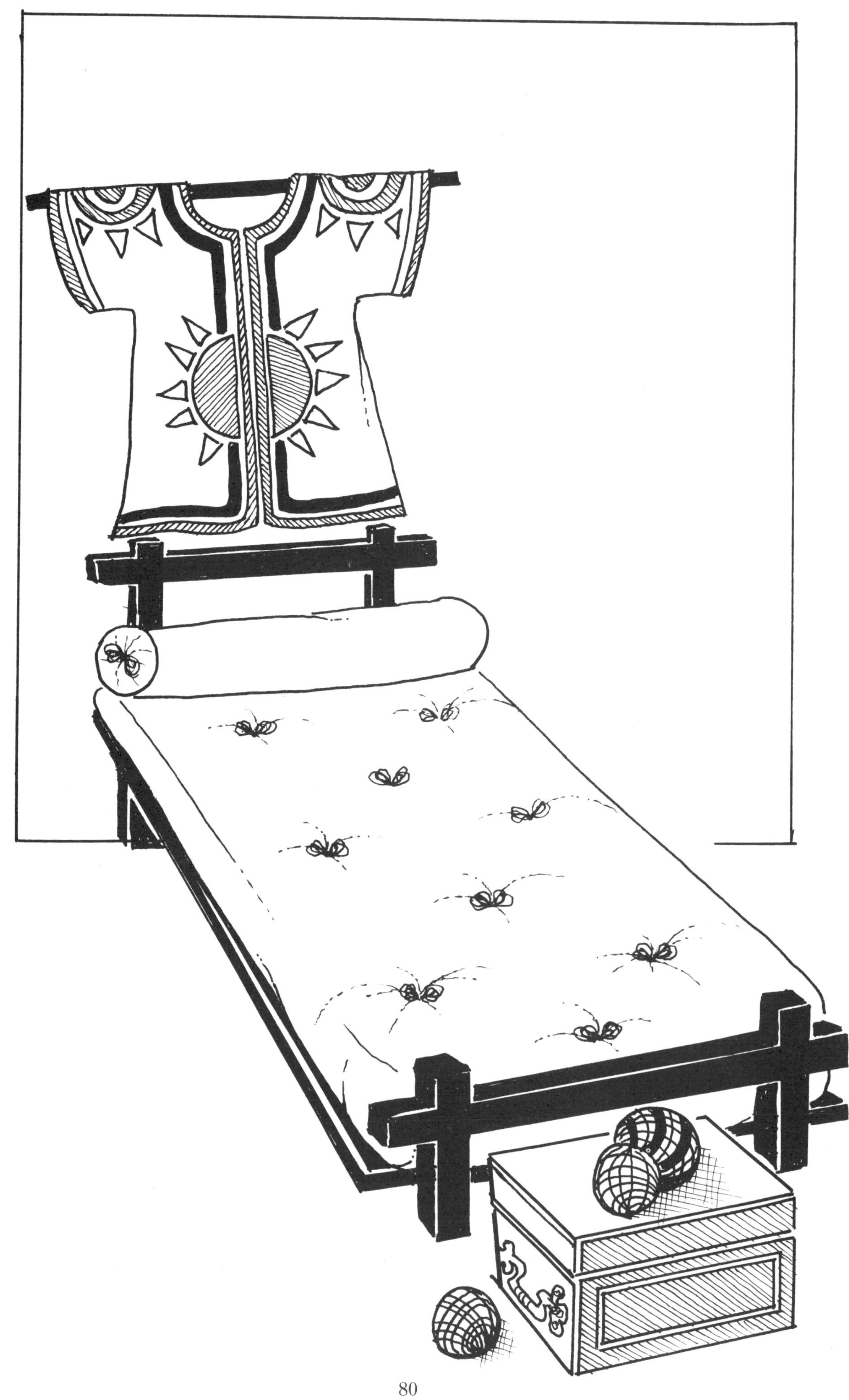

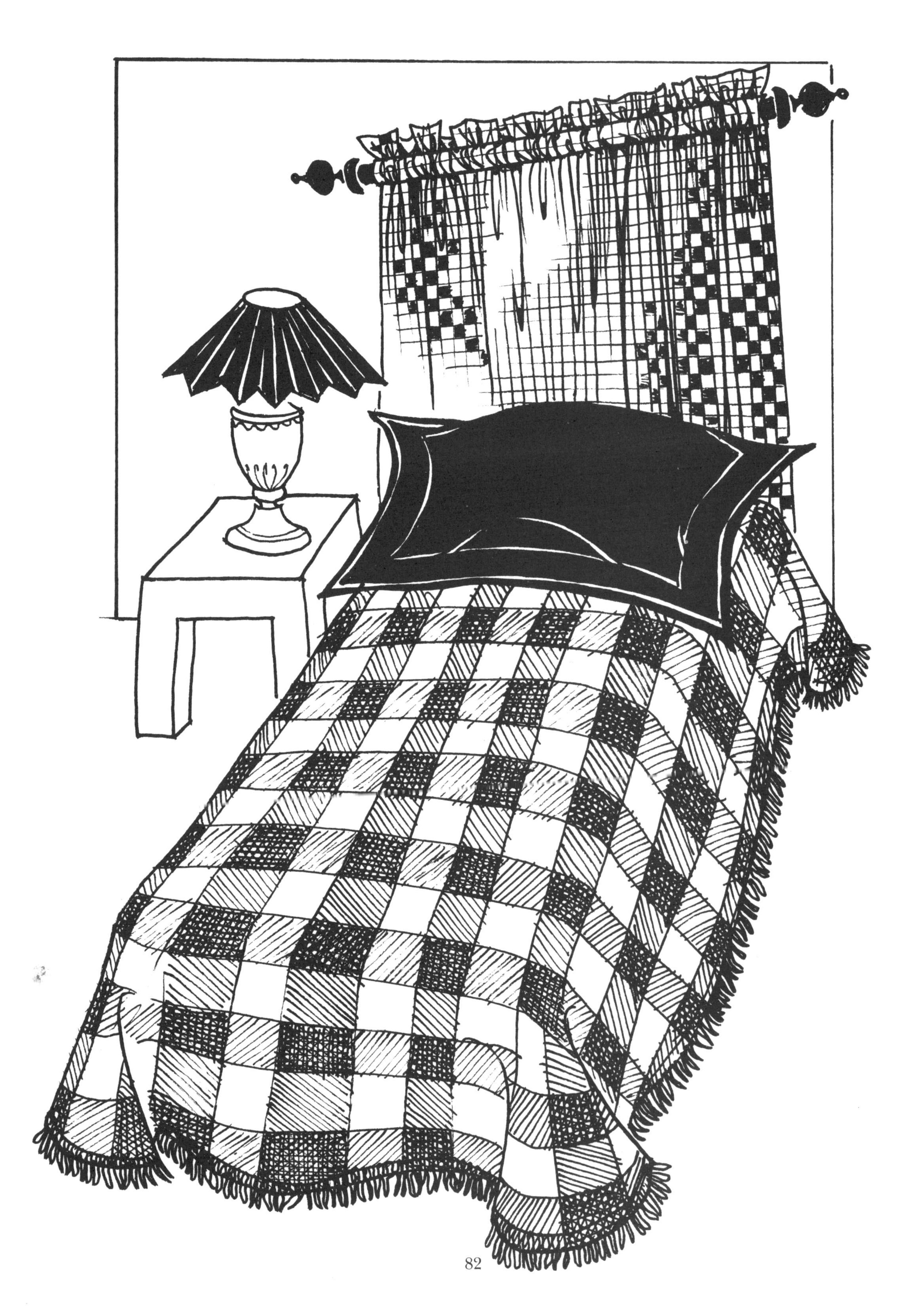

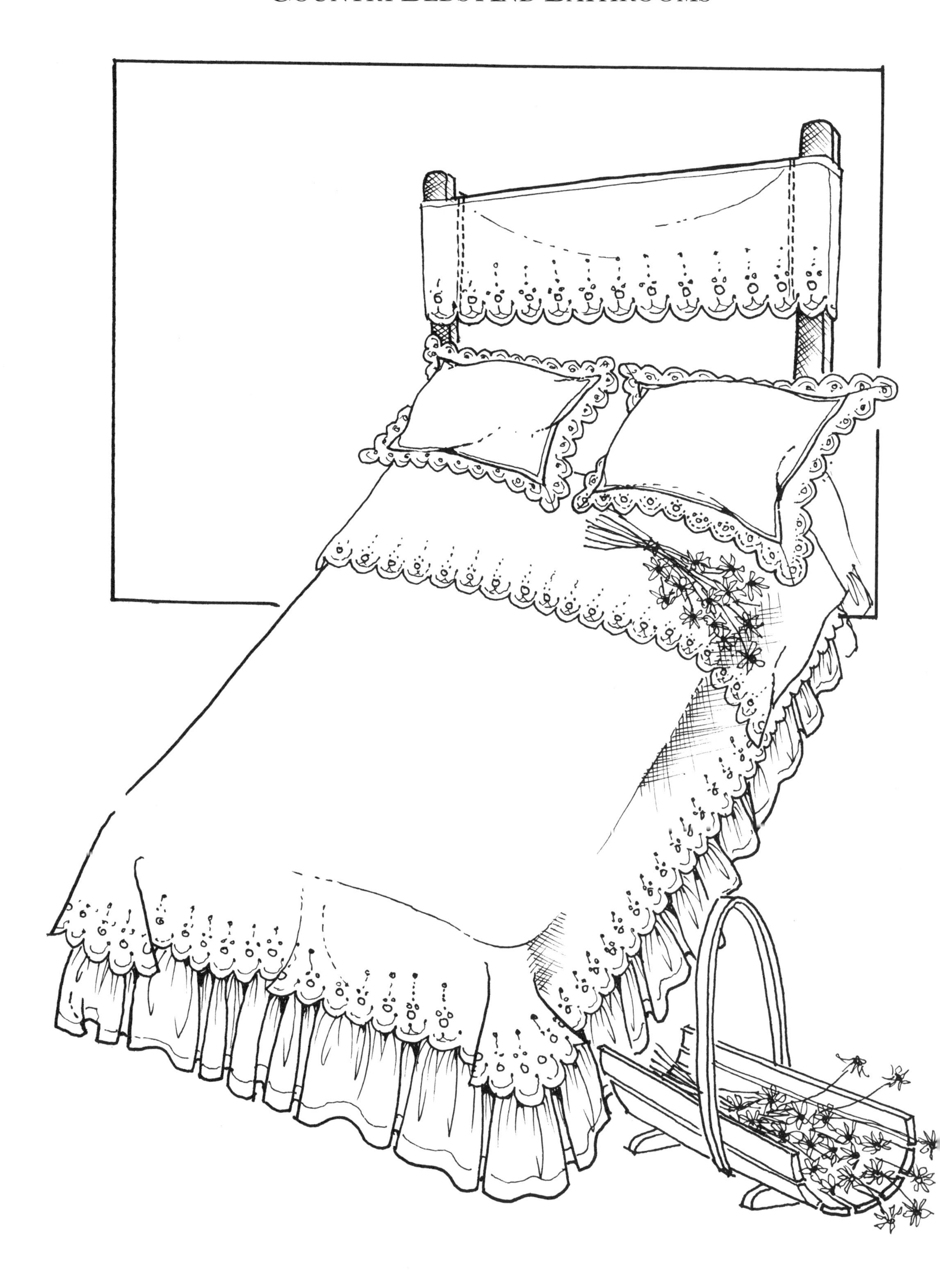

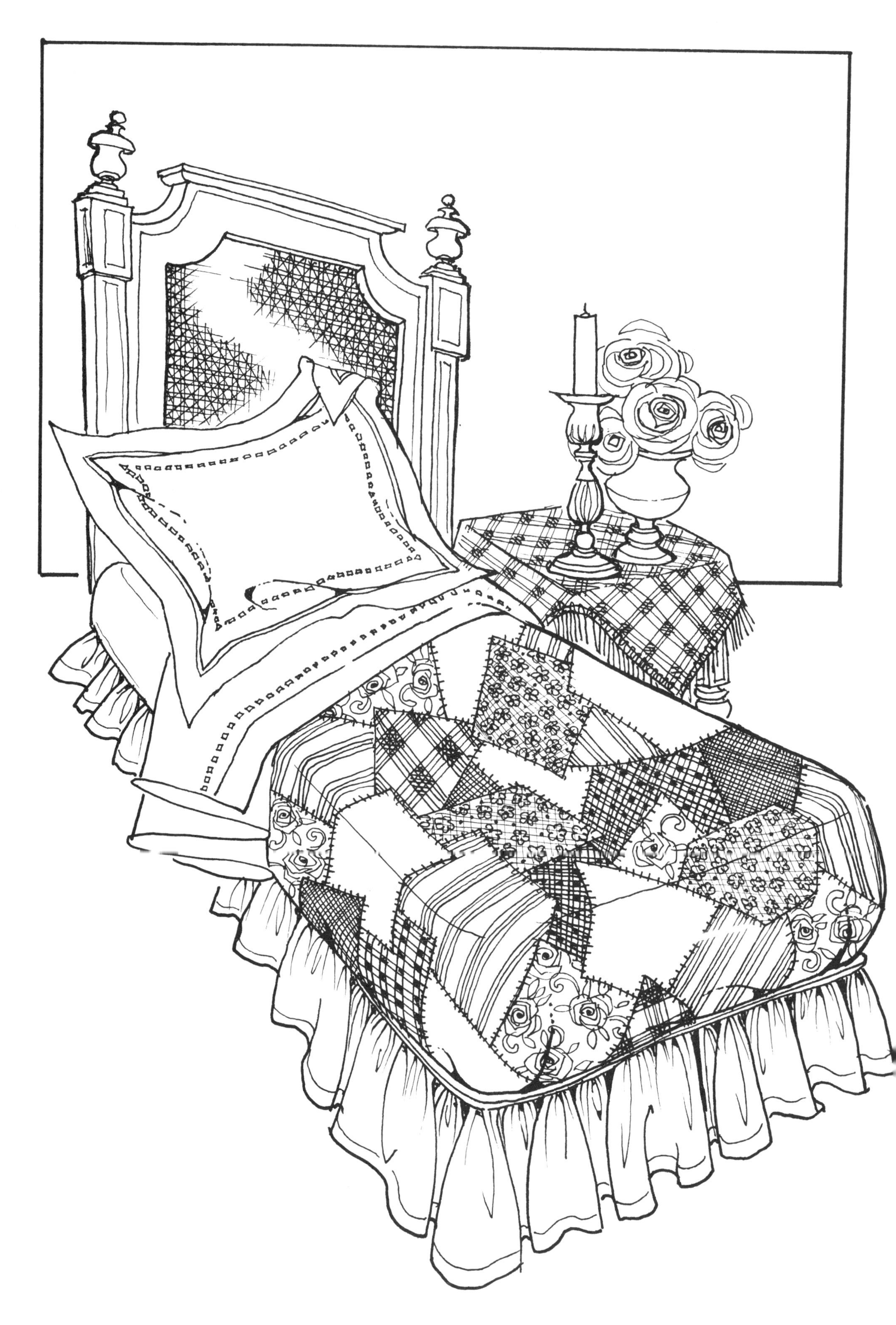

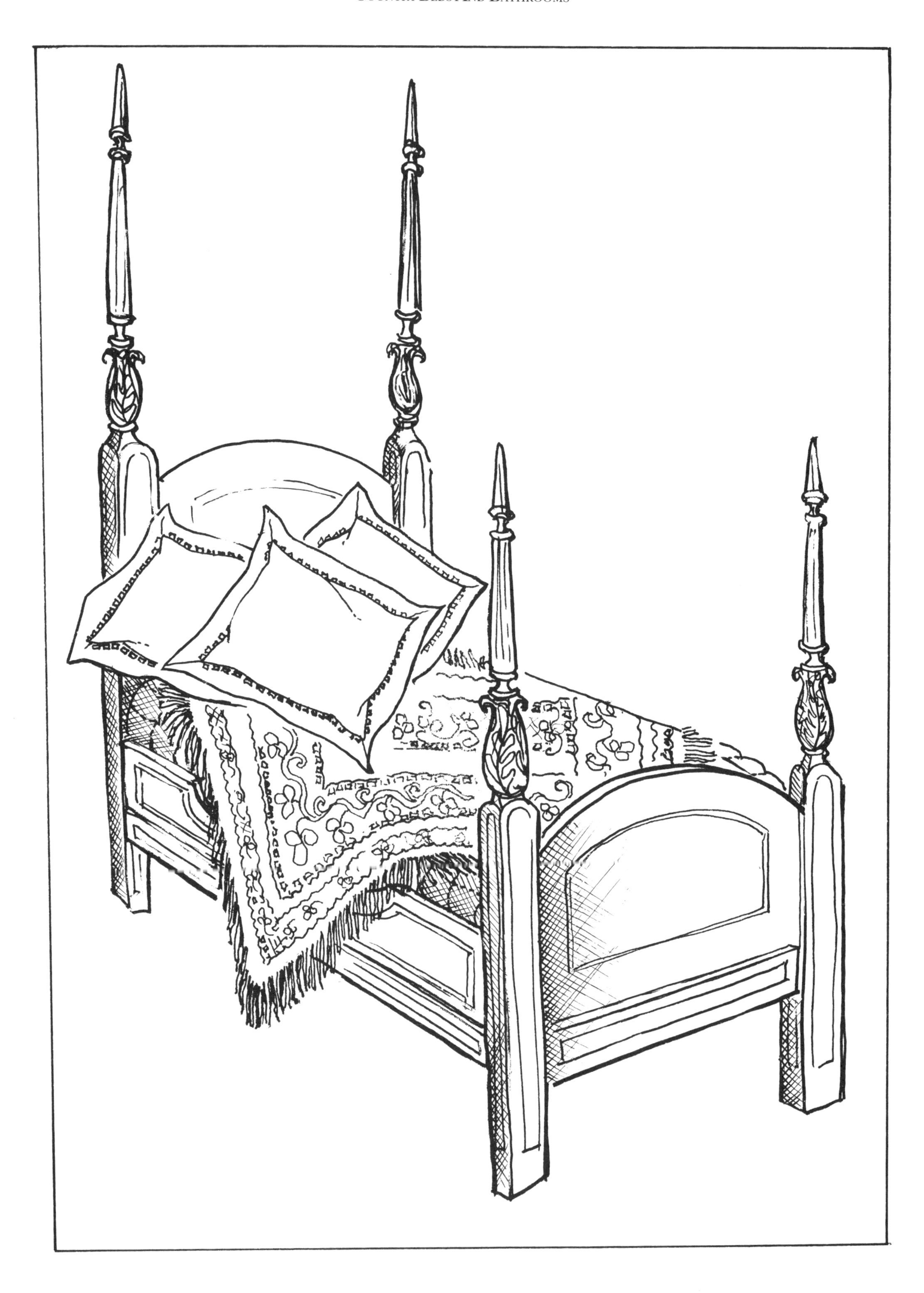

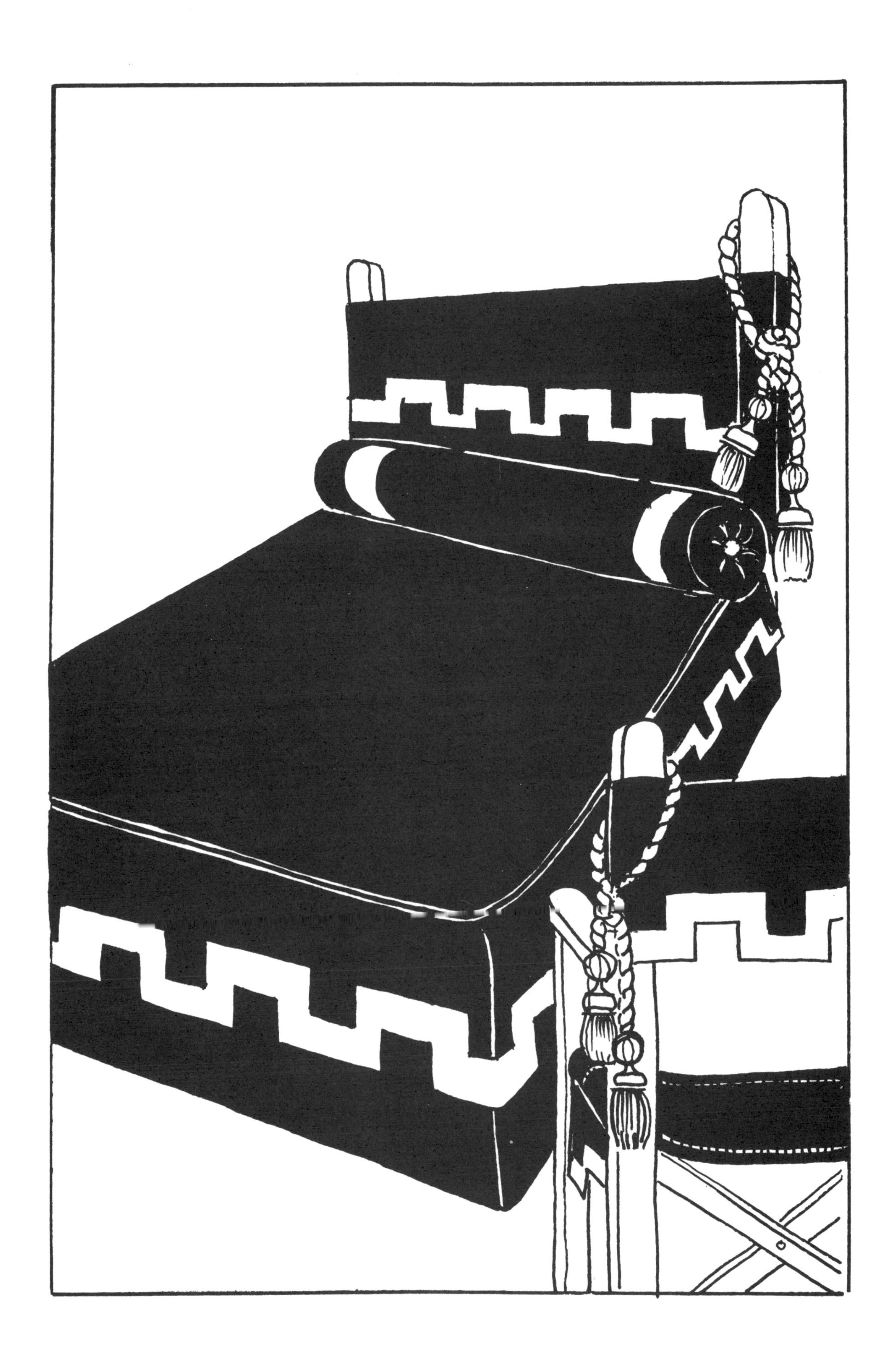

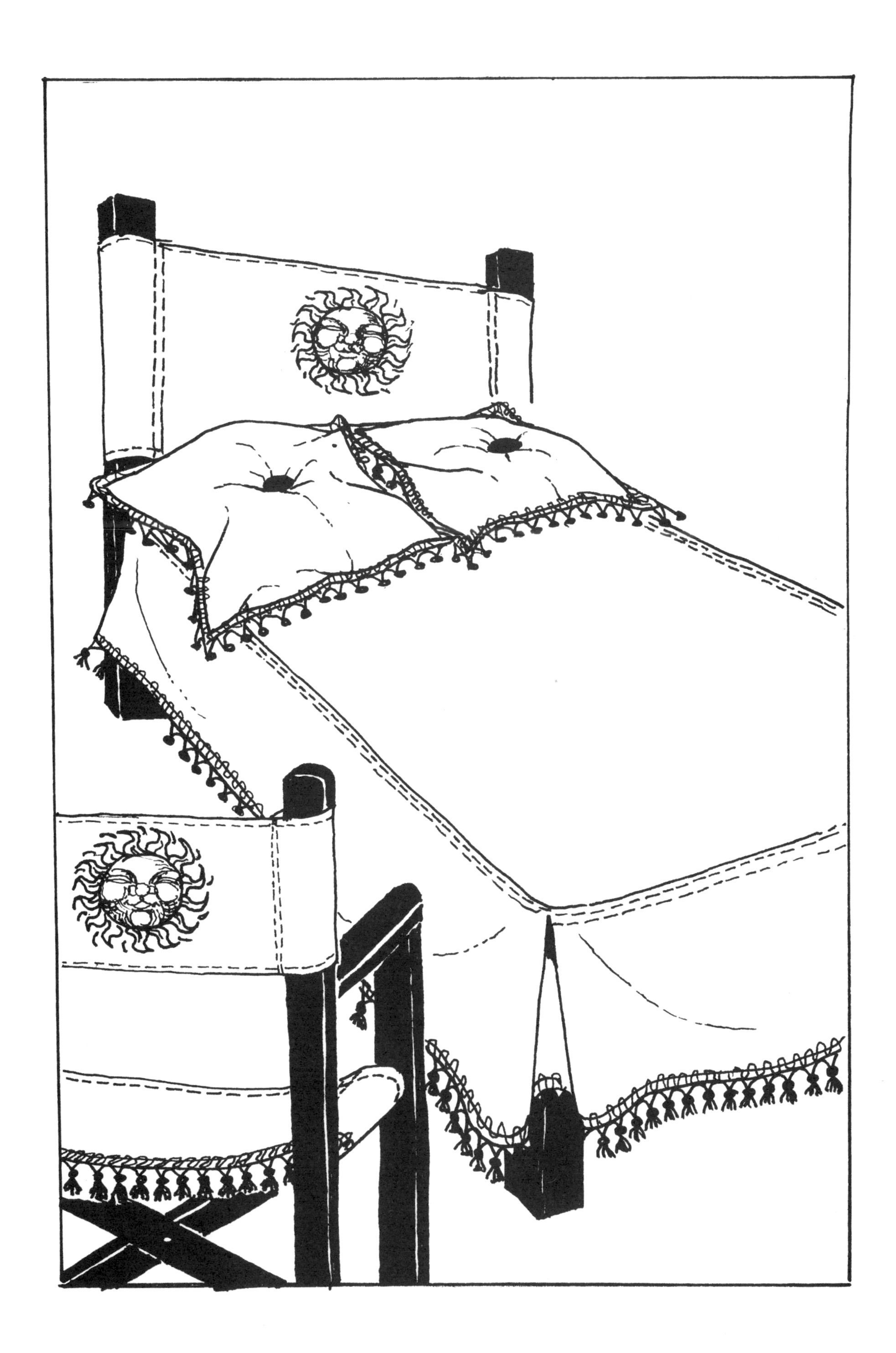

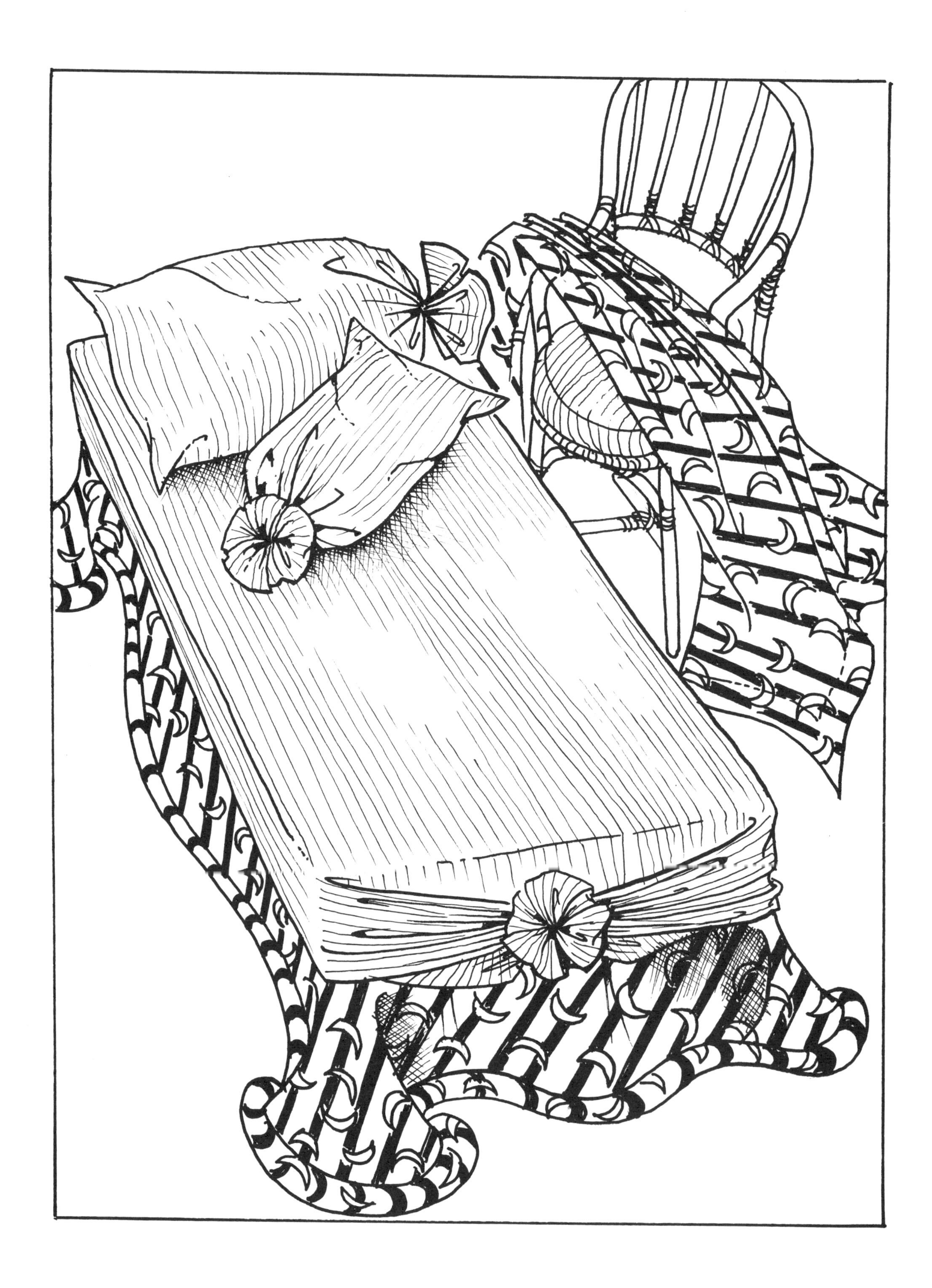

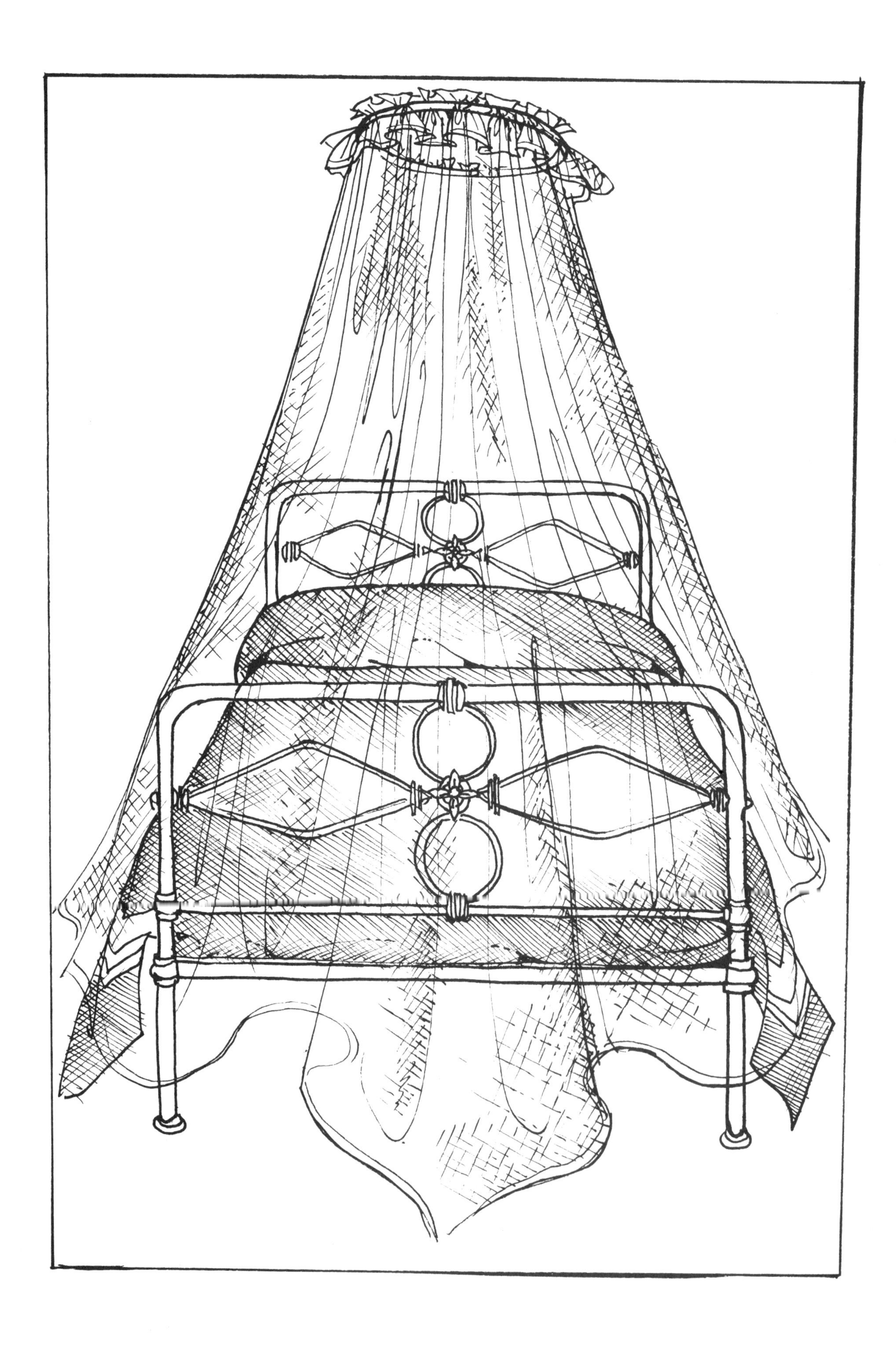

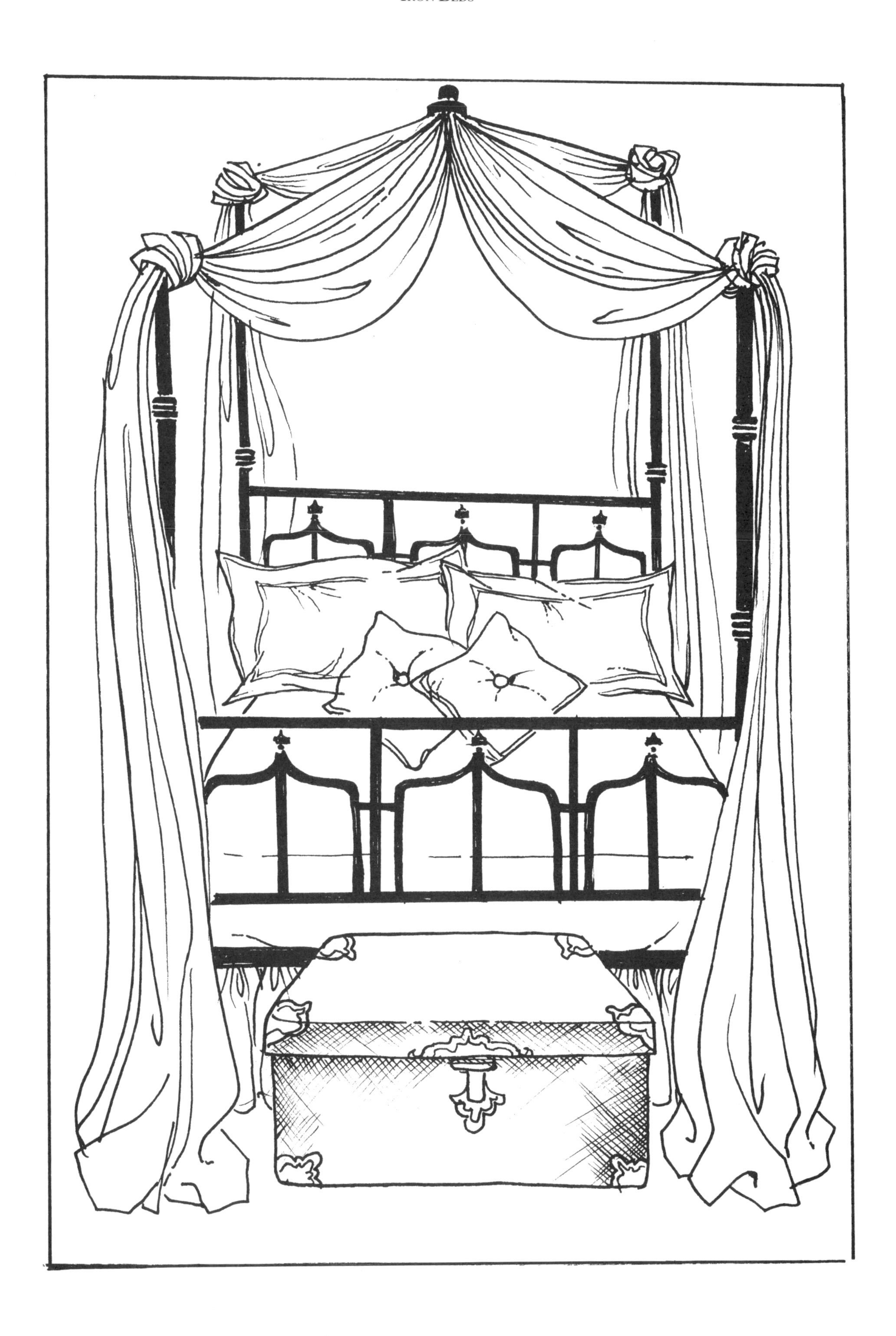

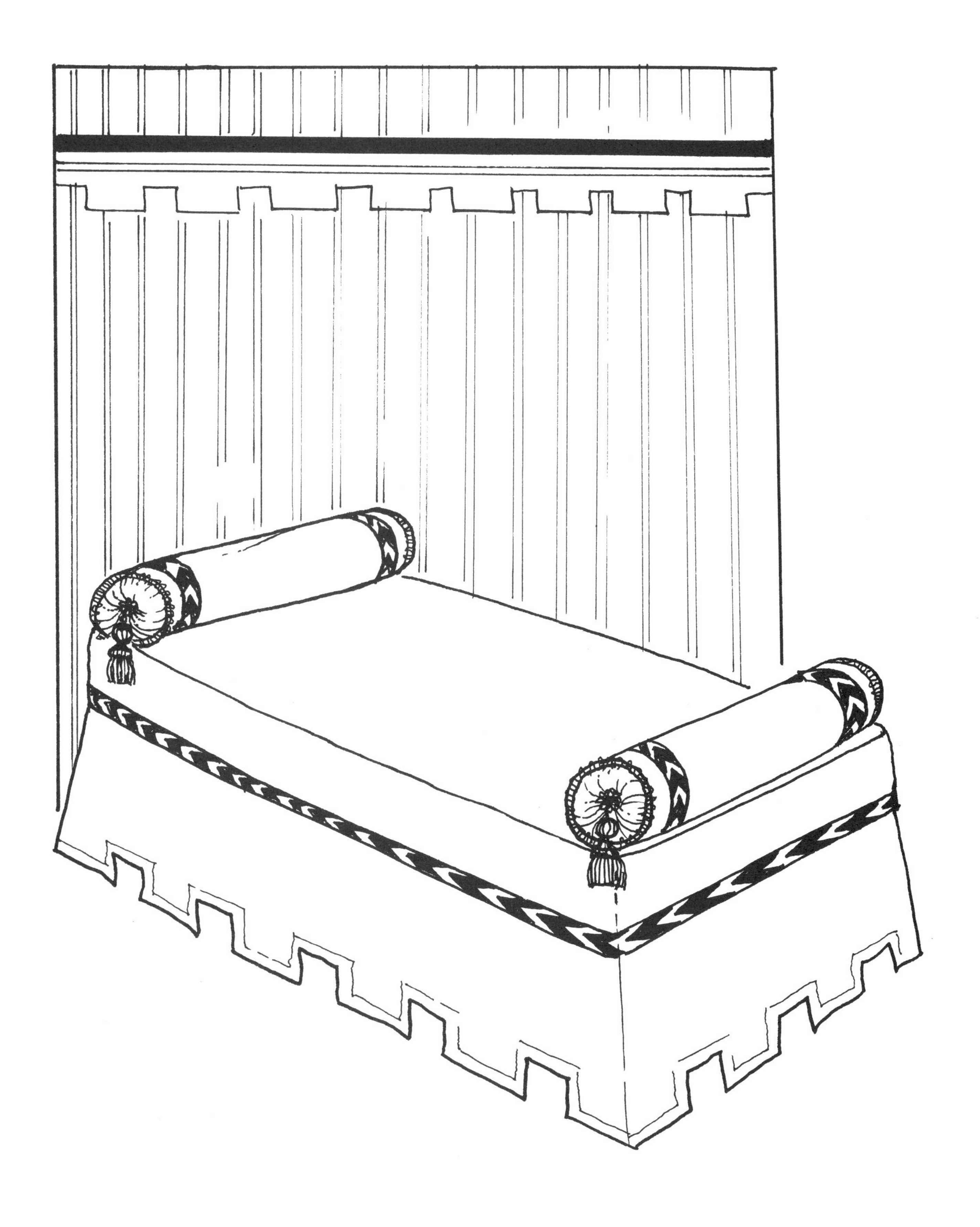

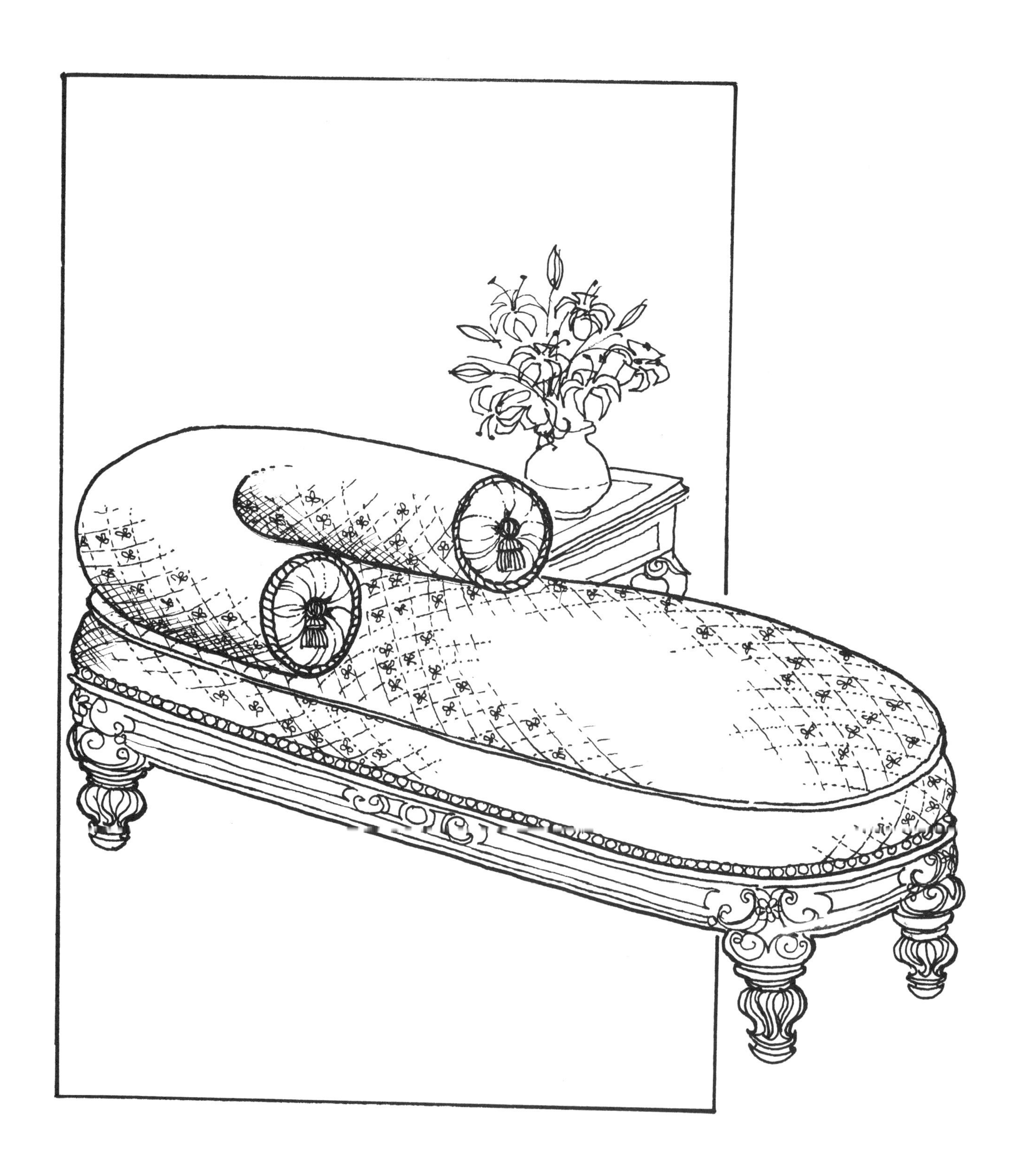

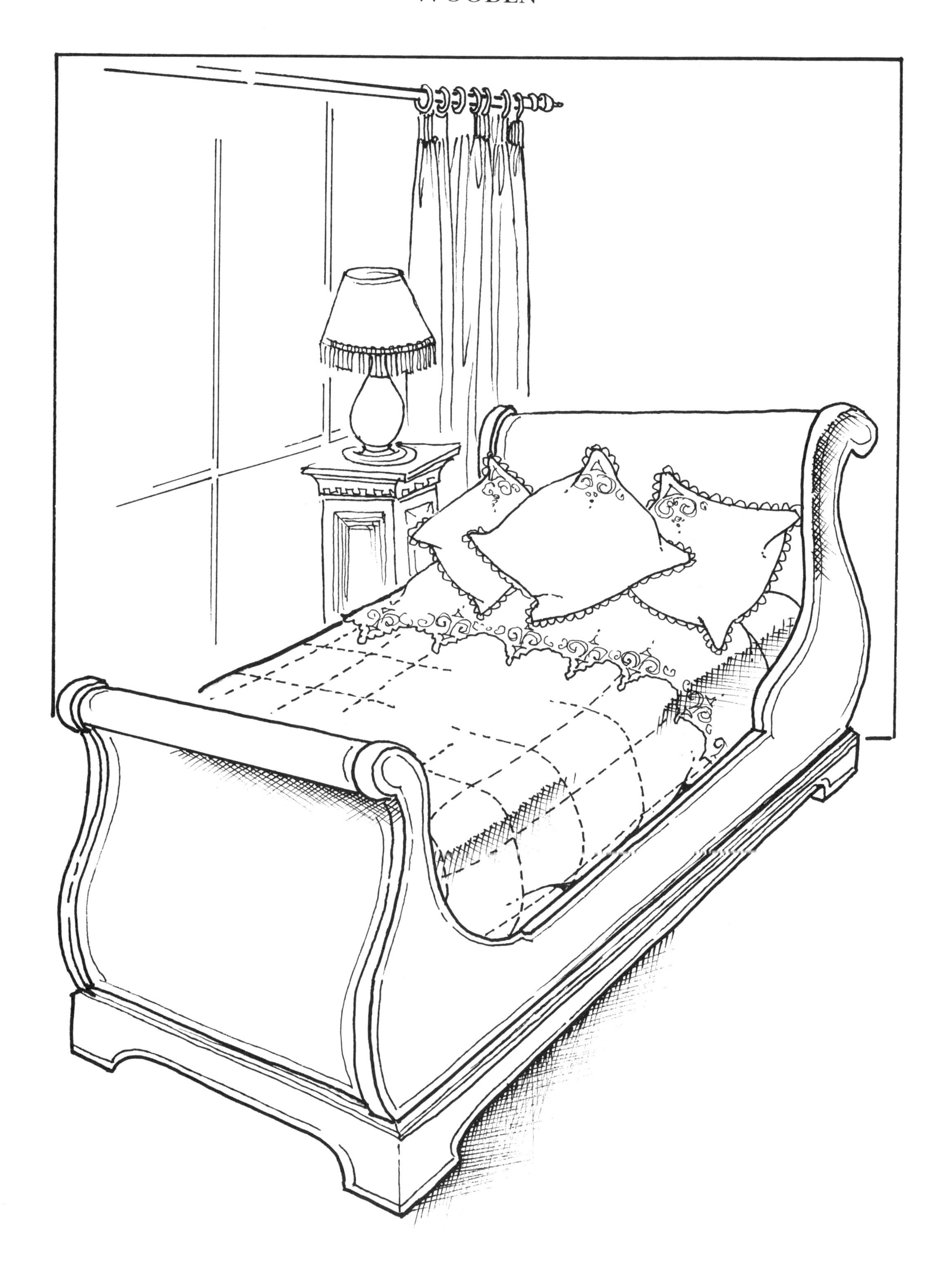

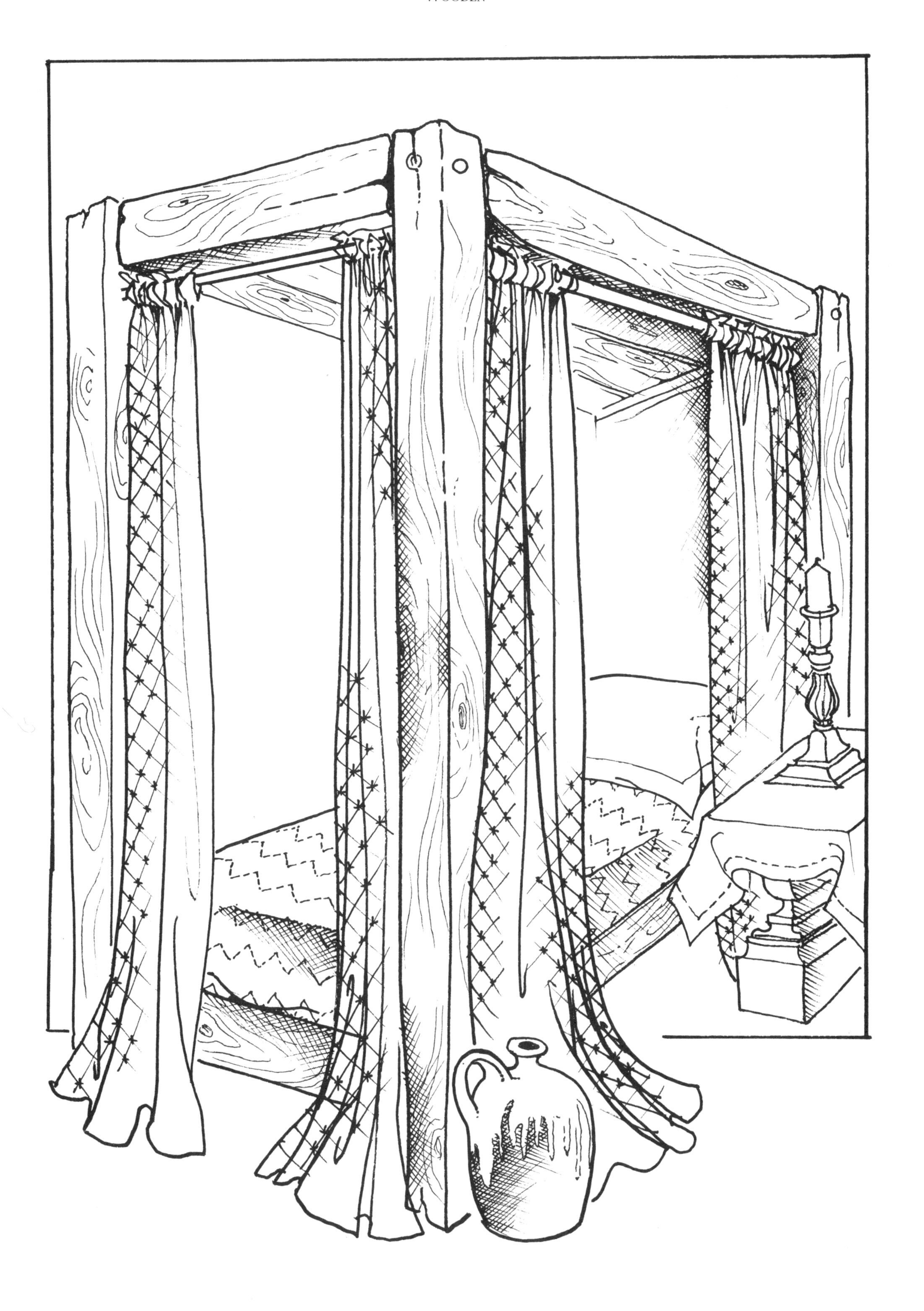

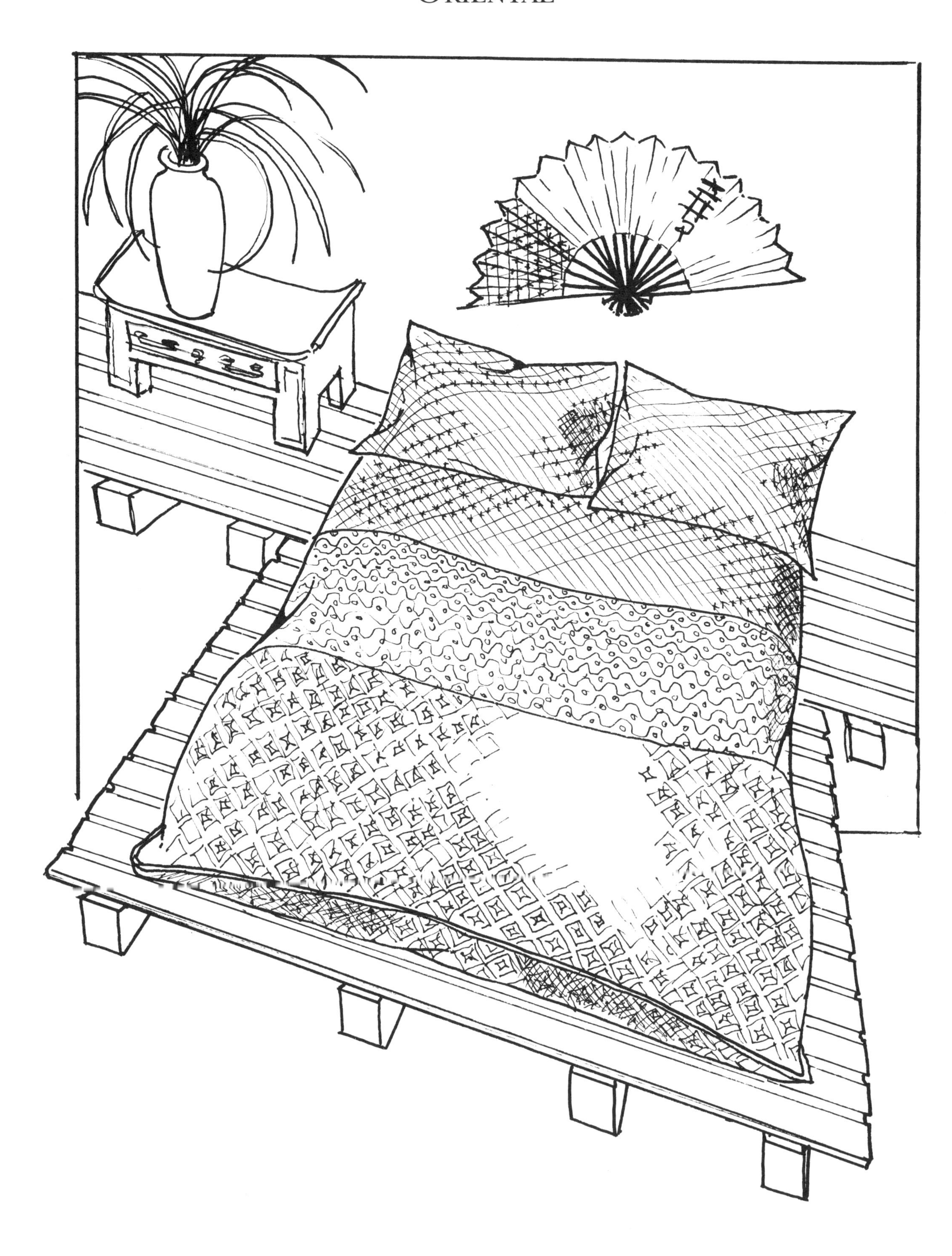

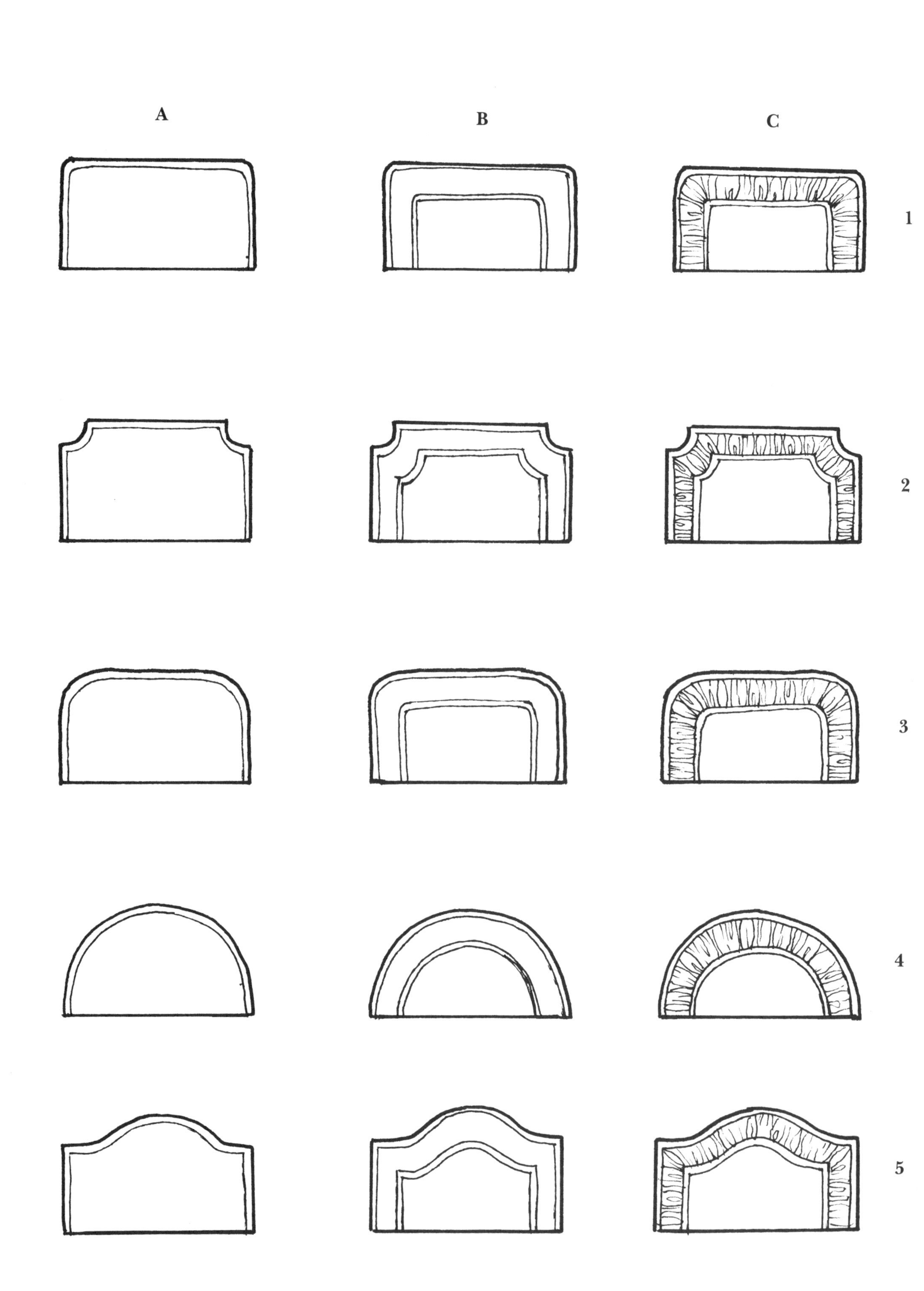
A
B
C
1
2
3
4
5

A
B
C
6
7
8
9
10

Basic Bed Covers

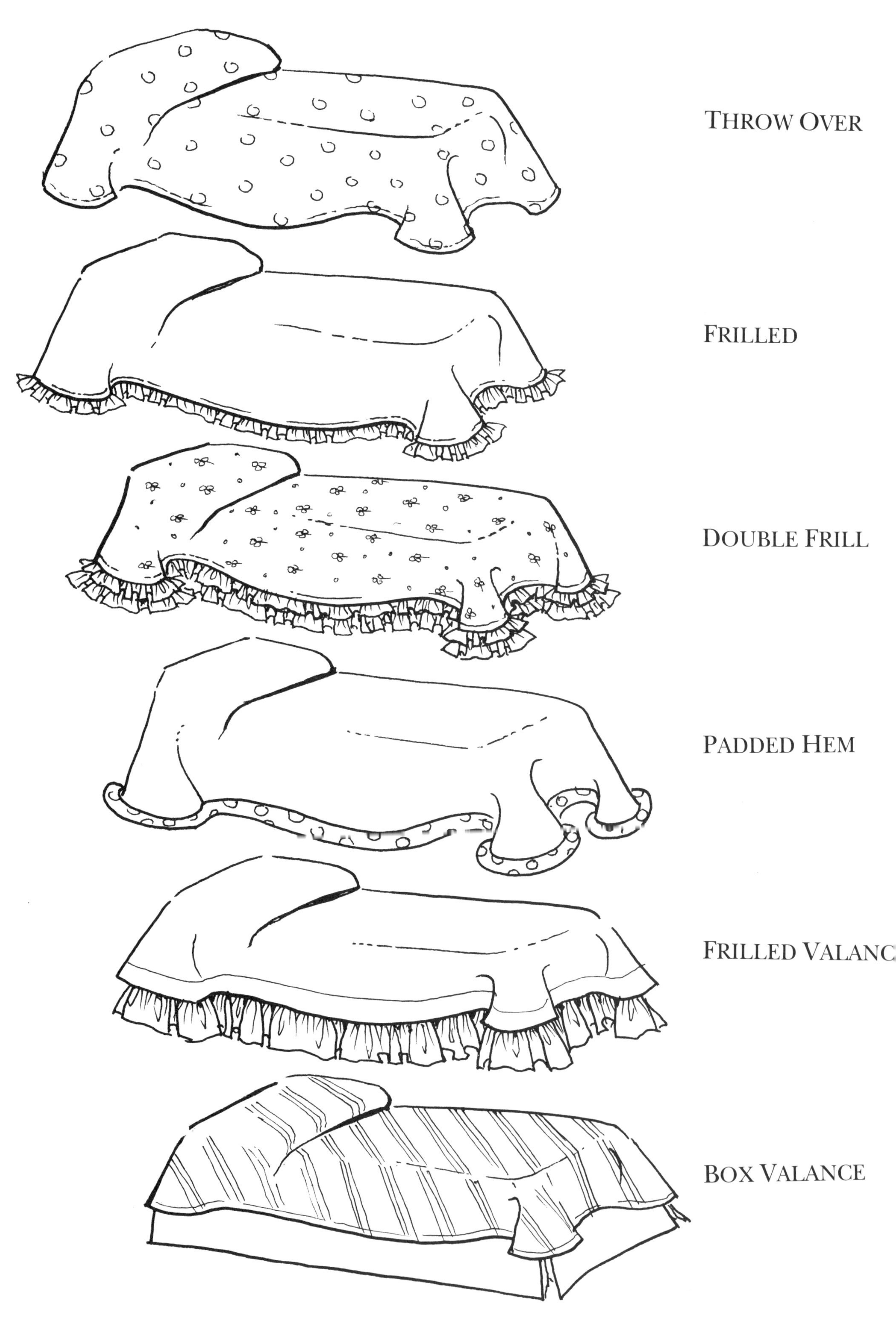

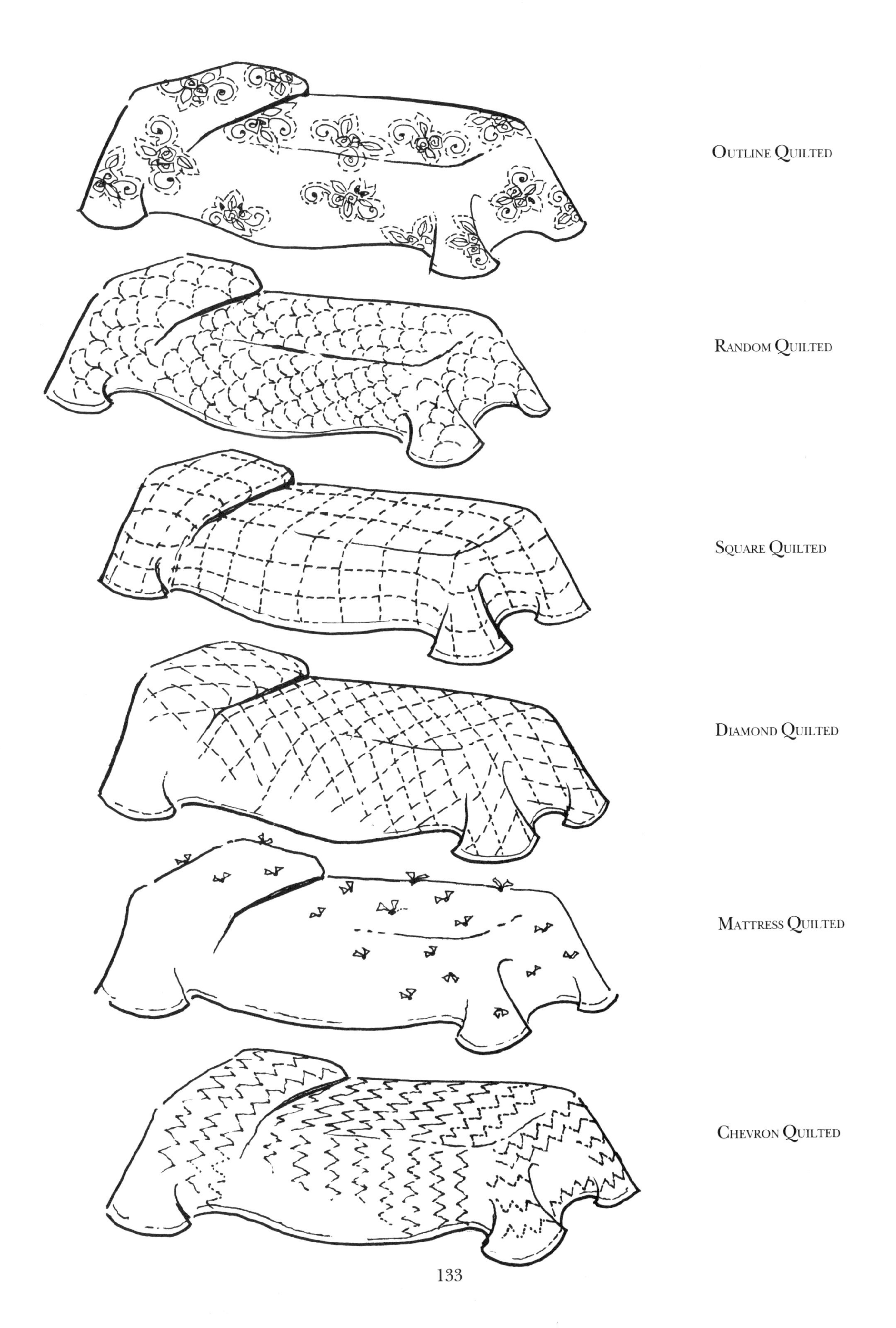
Outline Quilted
Random Quilted
Square Quilted
Diamond Quilted
Mattress Quilted
Chevron Quilted

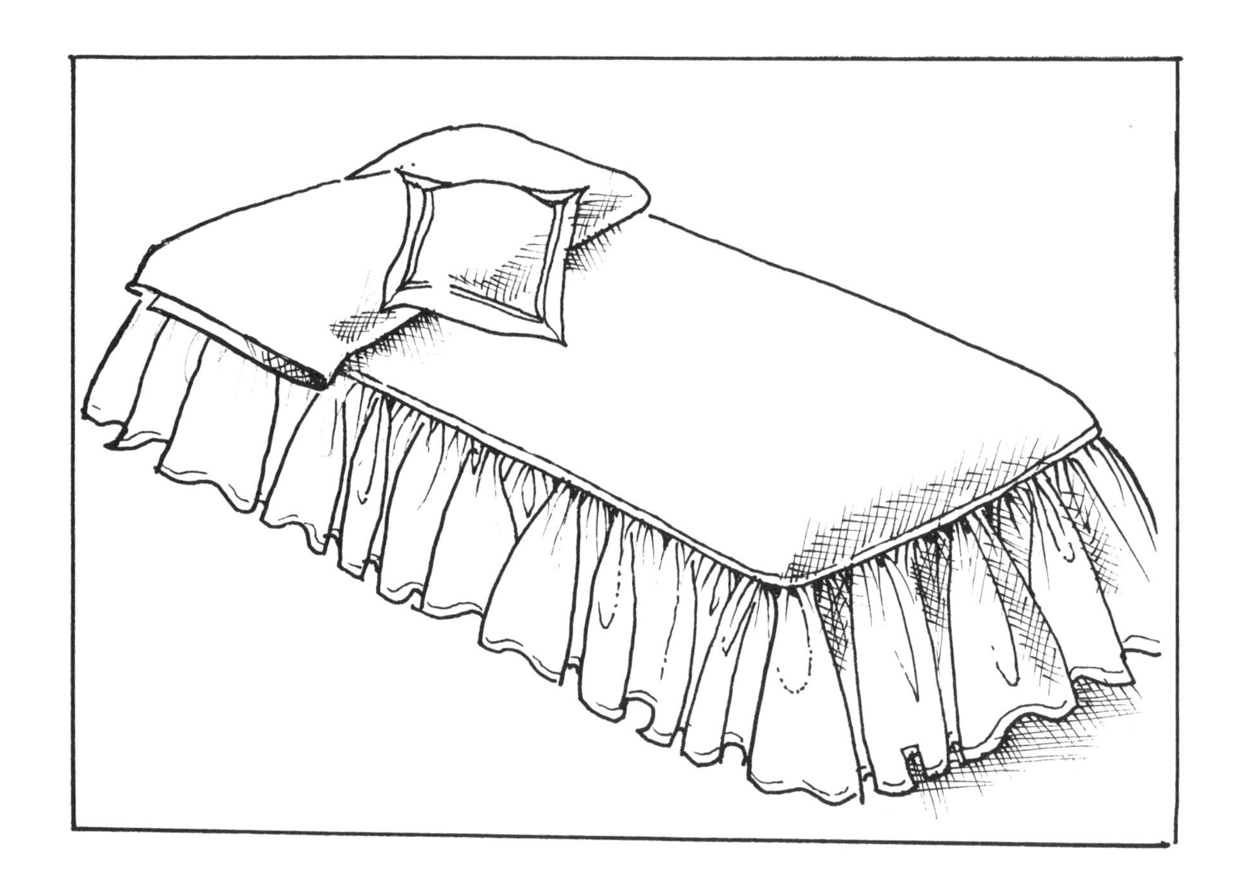

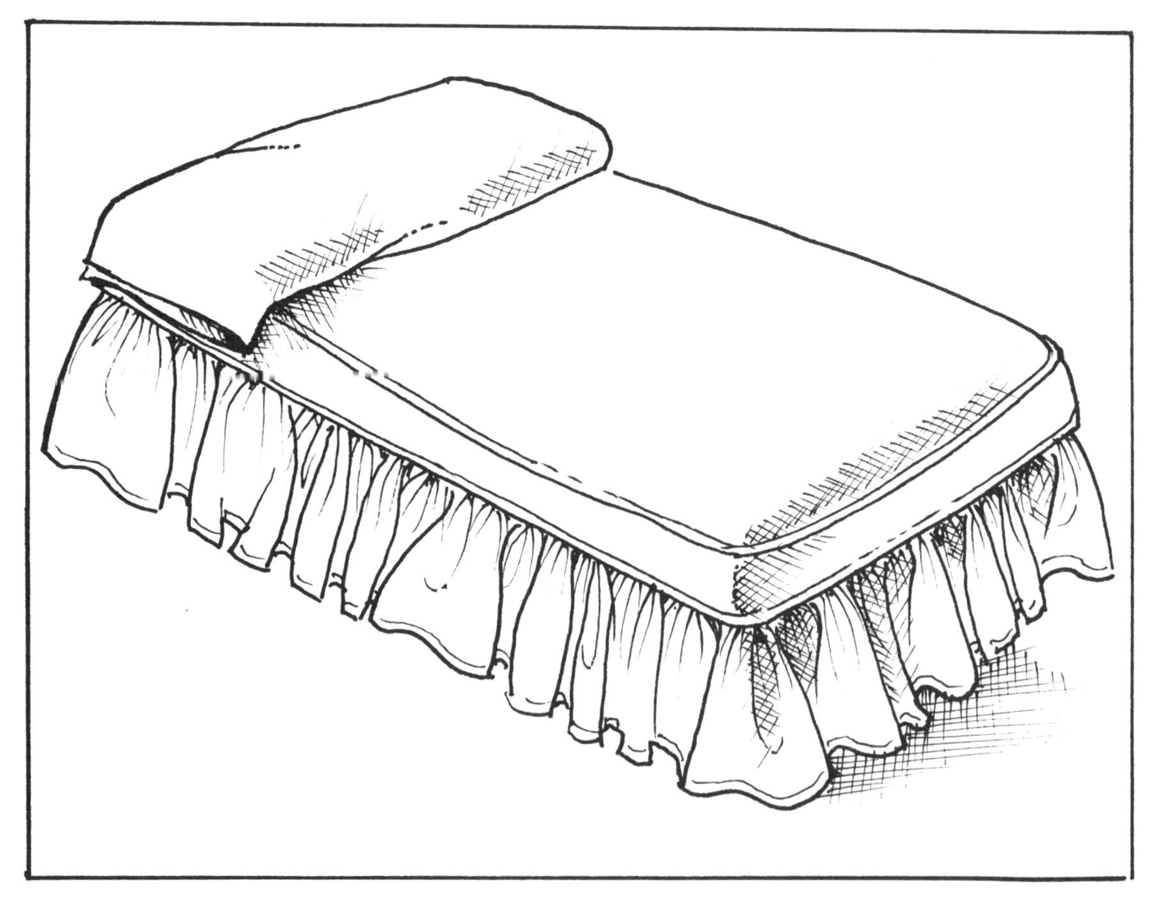

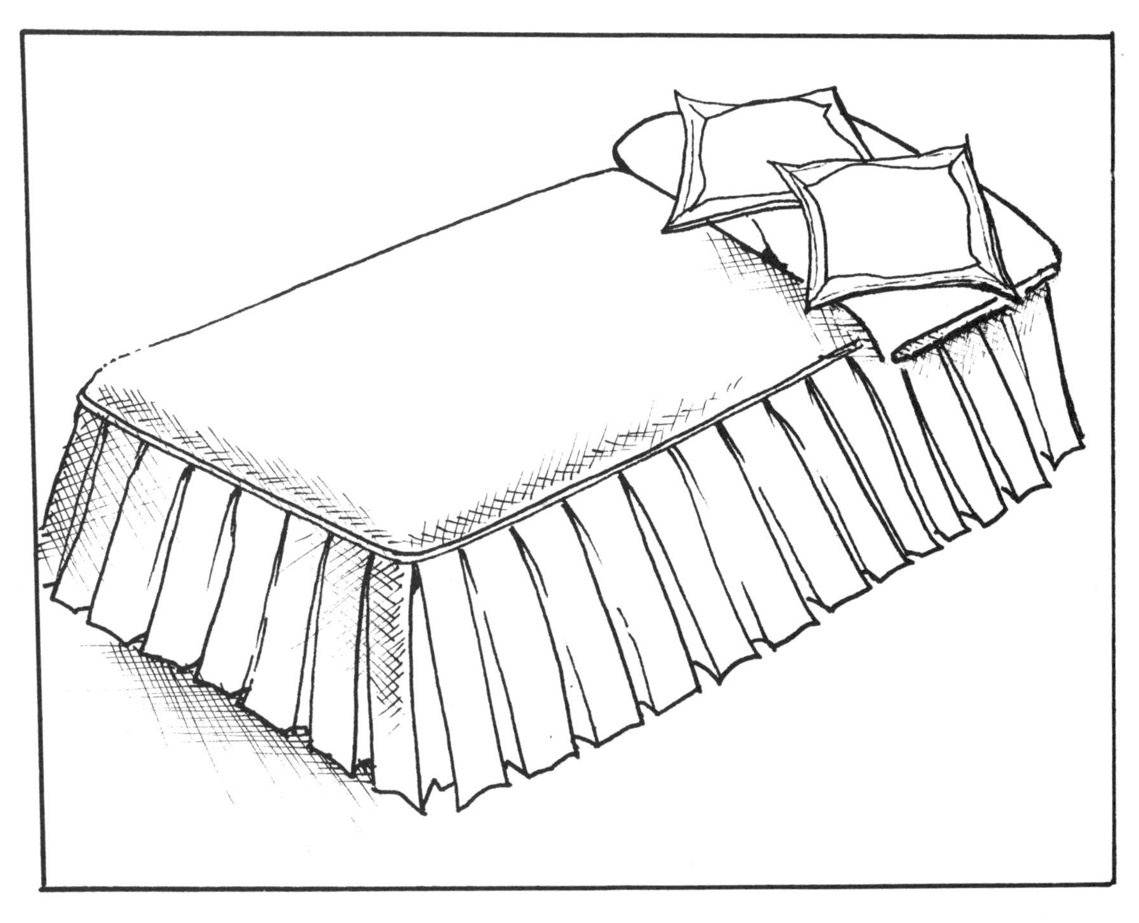

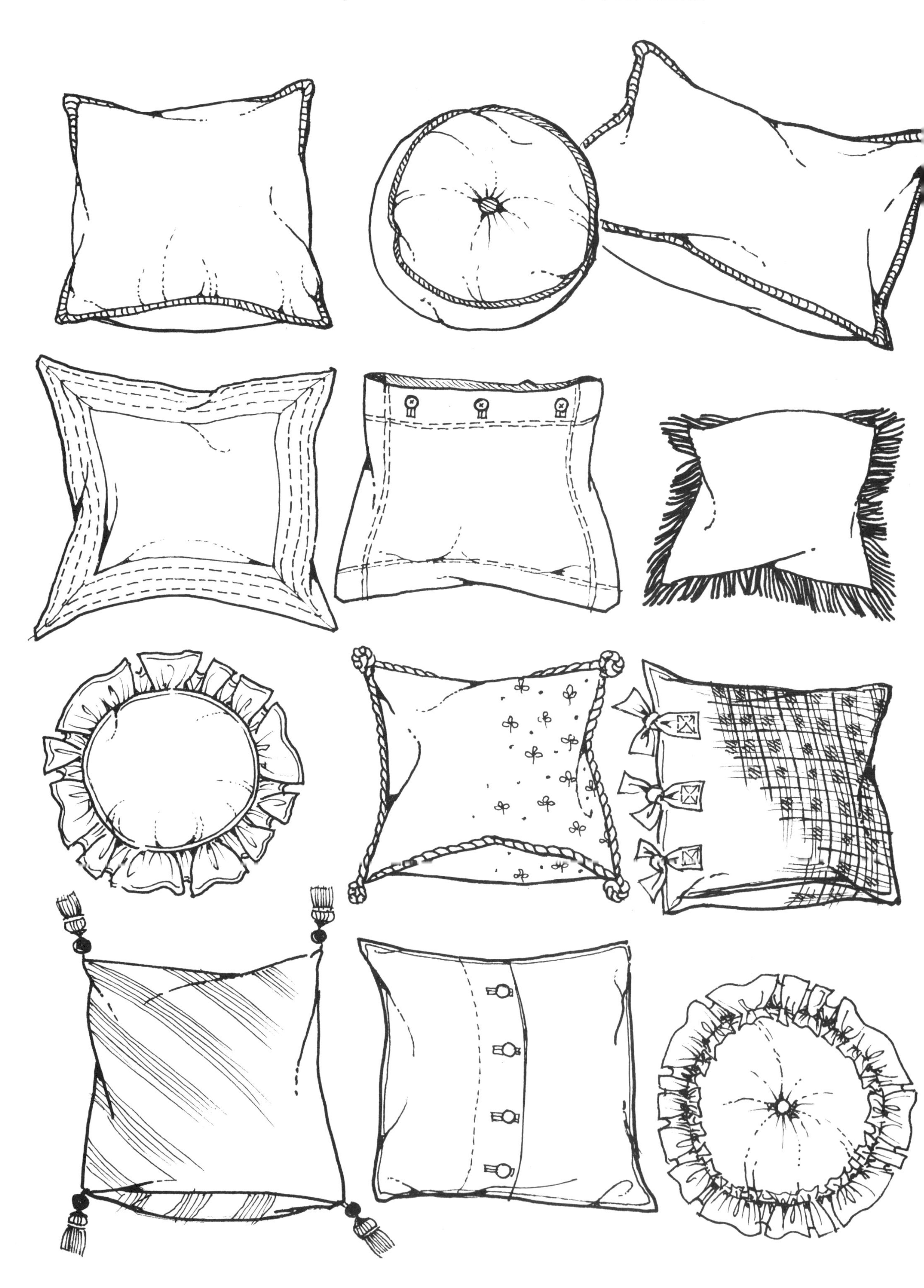

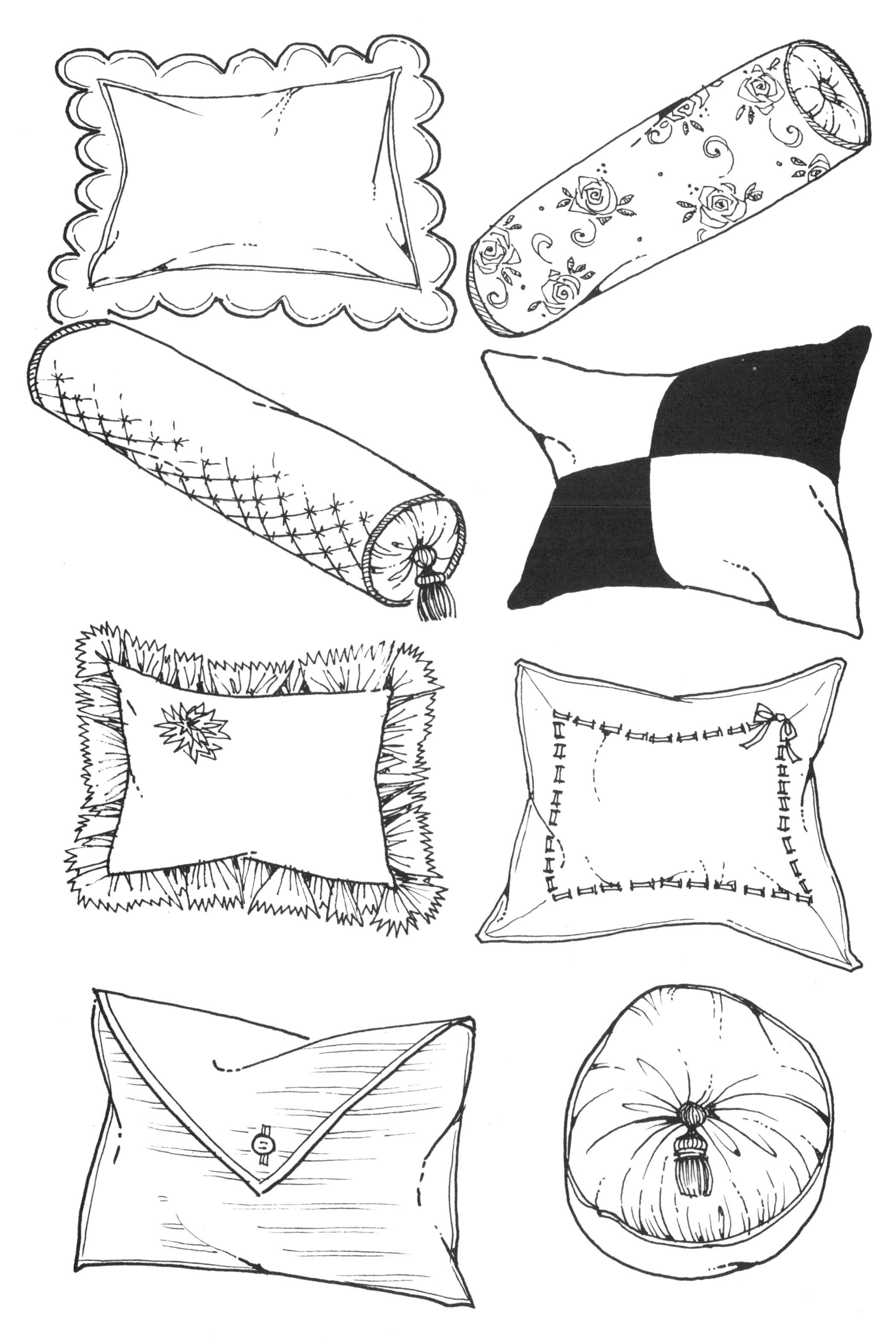

SUPPLIERS U.K.

FABRICS

OSBOURNE AND LITTLE,
(RETAIL)
304 KINGS ROAD,
LONDON SW3 5UH,
TEL: 0171 352 1456

JANE CHURCHILL,
(RETAIL)
151 SLOANE STREET,
LONDDON SW1X 9BZ.
TEL: 0171 730 6379/9847
FAX: 0171 259 9189

DECORATIVE FABRICS
GALLERY,
(RETAIL)
278-280 BROMPTON ROAD,
LONDON SW3 2AS.
TEL: 0171 589 4778
FAX: 0171 589 4781
(MONKWELL, FARDIS
G.P. & J BAKER, DESIGN
ARCHIVES, PARKATEX)

ANNA FRENCH,
(RETAIL)
343 KINGS ROAD,
LONDON SW3 5ES
TEL: 0171 351 1126

ANNA FRENCH,
(TRADE ONLY)
HEAD OFFICE,
108 SHAKESPEARE ROAD,
LONDON SW2 0QQ.
TEL: 0171 737 6555
FAX: 0171 274 8913

HILL AND KNOWLES,
(RETAIL)
133 KEW ROAD,
RICHMOND,
SURREY TW9 2PN.
TEL: 0181 948 4010

HILL AND KNOWLES,
(TRADE)
13 MOUNT STREET,
FELTHAM,
MIDDLESEX TW13 6AR.
TEL: 0181 893 3334
FAX: 0181 893 3850

JAB INTERNATIONAL,
(TRADE)
15-19 CAVENDISH PLACE,
LONDON W1 9DL.
TEL: 0171 636 2412
FAX: 0171 436 2412
(FABRICS AND VOILES)

TRIMMINGS

WENDY CUSHING,
(RETAIL)
UNIT M7,
CHELSEA GARDEN
MARKET,
CHELSEA HARBOUR,
LONDON SW10 0XE.
TEL: 0171 249 9709.
FAX: 0171 241 3441

TURNELL AND GIGON,
(RETAIL & TRADE)
UNIT M20,
CHELSEA GARDEN
MARKET,
CHELSEA HARBOUR,
LONDON SW 10 0XE.
TEL: 0171 351 5142
FAX: 0171 376 7945

JOHN LEWIS,
(DEPT STORE)
278-306 OXFORD STREET,
LONDON W1A IEX.
TEL: 0171 629 7711
FAX: 0171 629 0849
(FABRICS & TRIMMINGS,
INEXPENSIVE)

HEAD BOARDS, BEDSPREADS AND CUSHIONS

WENDY BAKER INTERIORS
THE OLD MALTHOUSE,
HAM,
MARLBOROUGH,
WILTSHIRE SN8 3RB.
TEL: 01488 668989
FAX: 01488 668818

JANE CHURCHILL,
151 SLOANE STREET,
LONDON SW1X 9BZ.
TEL: 0171 730 6379/9847
FAX: 0171 259 9189

DECORATIVE FABRICS
GALLERY,
278-280 BROMPTON ROAD,
LONDON SW3 2AS.
TEL: 0171 589 4778
FAX: 0171 589 4781

BED MANUFACTURERS

REYLON
STAPLES
DUNLOPILLOW
VI-SPRING
HYPNOS
(ALL OBTAINABLE AT
GOOD BED CENTRES AND
STORES)

MEDICAL BED SUPPLIES

JOHN BELL & CROYDON,
WIGMORE STREET,
LONDON WIH AOU
TEL: 0171 935 5555
FAX: 0171 935 9605

ORTHOPAEDIC BEDS

PARTNERS DIRECT,
42 CHURCH STREET,
REIGATE,
SURREY RH2 OAJ
TEL: 01737 226649
FAX: 01737 226659

PILLOWS ANDD SUPPORT PILLOWS

THE BACK SHOP,
24 NEW CAVENDISH
STREET,
LONDON W1M 7LH.
TEL: 0171 935 9120
FAX: 0171 224 1903

WOODEN BEDS

SIMON HORN,
(TRADE & RETAIL)
117-121 WANDSWORTH
BRIDGE ROAD,
LONDON SW6 2TP.
TEL: 0171 731 1279
FAX: 0171 736 3522

JOHN MINTER,
(RETAIL & TRADE)
GILLS GREEN,
HAWKHURST,
KENT TN18 5ER.
TEL: 0580 754499
FAX: 0580 754445
(SPECIALISTS IN
CHILDREN'S HAND-
PAINTED BEDROOM
FURNITURE)

IRON BEDS

BYGONE BEDS,
17 KING STREET,
SAFFRON WALDEN,
ESSEX CB10 1E
TEL: 01799 526000
FAX: 01799 584467
(SEND FOR CATALOGUE)

SO TO BED
638-640 KINGS ROAD,
LONDON SW6 2DU.
TEL: 0171 731 3593
FAX: 0171 371 5272
(WORTH A VISIT)

BED LINEN AND PILLOWS

JOHN LEWIS
PARTNERSHIP,
278-306 OXFORD STREET,
LONDON W1A IEX.
TEL: 0171 629 7711
FAX: 0171 629 0849
(STORES THROUGHOUT U.K.)

HARRODS,
BROMPTON ROAD,
KNIGHTSBRIDGE,
LONDON SW1X 7XL.
TEL: 0171 730 1234
FAX: 0171 581 0470

THE CONRAN SHOP,
MICHELIN HOUSE,
81 FULHAM ROAD,
LONDON SW3 6RD.
TEL: 0171 589 7401
FAX: 0171 823 7015

HABITAT,
208 KINGS ROAD,
LONDON SW3 5XP.
TEL: 0171 351 1211
FAX: 0171 351 4249
(ALSO SELECTION OF BEDS
IN BRANCHES
THROUGHOUT U.K.)

THE WHITE HOUSE,
51-52 NEW BOND STREET,
LONDON W1Y 0BY.
TEL: 0171 629 3521
FAX: 0171 629 8269

FRETTE,
98 NEW BOND STREET,
LONDON W1Y 9LF.
TEL: 0171 491 2750
FAX: 0171 499 2332
(LOVELY BUT EXPENSIVE)

DAMASK,
3-4 BROXHOLME HOUSE,
NEW KINGS ROAD,
LONDON SW6 4AA.
TEL: 0171 731 3553
FAX: 0171 731 3553
(ALSO PATCHWORK QUILTS)

LUNN ANTIQUES,
86 NEW KINGS ROAD,
LONDON SW6 4LV
TEL: 0171 736 4638
FAX: 0171 371 7113
(ANTIQUE BED LINENS)

BATHROOM SUPPLIERS

SITTING PRETTY,
(RETAIL & TRADE)
131 DAWES ROAD,
LONDDON SW6 7EA
TEL: 0171 381 0049
FAX: 0171 385 9621

C.P.HART,
(RETRAIL & TRADE)
NEWHAM TERRACE,
LONDON SE1 7DR.
TEL: 0171 928 5866
FAX: 0171 902 1001

ORIGINAL BATHROOMS,
(RETAIL & TRADE)
143-145 KEW ROAD,
RICHMOND,
SURREY TW9 2PN.
TEL: 0181 940 7554
FAX: 0181 948 8200

DRESSING TABLES AND PADDED MIRRORS

WENDY BAKER INTERIORS,
THE OLD MALTHOUSE,
HAM,
MARLBOROUGH,
WILTSHIRE SN8 3RB.
TEL: 01488 668989
FAX: 01488 668818

SUPPLIERS U.S.A.

FABRICS

BRUNSCHWIG & FILS,
979 3RD AVENUE,
NEW YORK.
TEL: (212) 838 7878

HINSON & CO. (SHEERS)·
979 3RD AVENUE,
NEW YORK, 10022.
TEL: (212) 688 5538

OSBOURNE & LITTLE,
(TRADE ONLY)
SUITE 520,
979 3RD AVENUE,
NEW YORK, 10022.
TEL: (212) 751 3333
FAX: (212) 752 6027

OSBOURNE & LITTLE,
(TRADE ONLY)
SUITE 520,
610 MERCHANDISE MART,
IL 60654.
TEL: (312) 467 0913
FAX: (312) 467 0996

SCALAMANDRE,
950 3RD AVENUE,
NEW YORK, 10022.
TEL: (212) 415 3900

SCHUMACHER,
939 3RD AVENUE,
NEW YORK, 10022.
TEL: (212) 415 3900
(ALSO TRIMMINGS)

BED MANUFACTURERS

MAJESTIC MATTRESS CO.,
361 MAIN STREET,
WAREHAM,
MASSACHUSETTS 02571
TEL: (508) 295 7615

OTHER NAMES TO LOOK FOR:
SEALY
SERTA
SHIFMAN
SPRINGAIR
SIMMONS
STERN & FOSTER
(AVAILABLE FROM MOST MAJOR STORES THROUGHOUT THE U.S.A.)

BED LINEN

BED, BATH & BEYOND,
620 6TH AVENUE,
NEW YORK.
TEL: (212) 255 3550
(BRANCHES THROUGHOUT U.S.A)

BLOOMINGDALES,
59TH & LEXINGTON AVENUE,
NEW YORK.
TEL: (212) 705 2000
FAX: (212) 705 2076

E. BRAUN & CO,
717 MADISON AVENUE,
NEW YORK.
TEL: (212) 838 0650

FRETTE,
799 MADISON AVENUE,
NEW YORK.
TEL: (212) 988 5221

MACY'S
HERALD SQUARE,
151 WEST 34TH STREET,
NEW YORK.
TEL: (212) 695 4400

PORTHAULT,
18 EAST 69TH STREET,
NEW YORK.
TEL: (212) 249 8361

PRATESI LINENS,
829 MADISON AVENUE,
NEW YORK.
TEL: (212) 288 2315

SCHWEITZER LINENS,
1132 MADISON AVENUE,
NEW YORK.
TEL: (212) 249 [illegible]

CUSTOM MADE BEDS

CHAS H. BECKLEY INC.,
306 EAST 61ST STREET,
NEW YORK.
TEL: (212) 759 8450

BATHROOM SUPPLIERS

ELGOT,
937 LEXINGTON AVENUE,
NEW YORK.
TEL: (212) 879 1200

GRACIOUS HOME,
1220 3RD AVENUE,
NEW YORK.
TEL: (212) 517 6300

(LOOK OUT FOR MANUFACTURERS AMERICAN STANDARD & KOHLER)

HEADBOARDS

ABC CARPET & HOME,
888 BROADWAY,
NEW YORK.
TEL: (212) 473 3000

AVERY BOARDMAN,
(TRADE ONLY)
979 3RD AVENUE,
NEW YORK.
TEL: (212) 688 6611

BLOOMINGDALES
(RETAIL)
59TH & LEXINGTON AVENUE,
NEW YORK.
TEL: (212) 705 2000
FAX: (212) 705 2076

HAMILTON FURNITURE,
107 EAST 63RD STREET,
NEW YORK, 10021.
TEL: (212) 826 0826

WOODEN, IRON & BRASS BEDS

ALICE'S ANTIQUES,
505 COLUMBUS AVENUE,
NEW YORK.
TEL: (212) 874 3400

ANGLO INDIAN FURNITURE,
62 GREENE STREET,
NEW YORK, 10012.
TEL: (212) 343 2299

BLOOMINGDALES,
59TH & LEXINGTON AVENUE,
NEW YORK.
TEL: (212) 705 2000
FAX: (212 705 2076)

ETHAN ALLEN,
192 LEXINGTON AVENUE,
NEW YORK.
TEL: (212) 213 0600

GRANGE,
200 LEXINGTON AVENUE,
NEW YORK, 10016.
TEL: (212) 685 9057
(WOODEN & SLEIGH BEDS)

MACY'S ,
HERALD SQUARE,
151 WEST 34TH STREET,
NEW YORK.
TEL: (212) 695 4400.

CHARLES P. ROGERS,
899 1ST AVENUE,
NEW YORK.
TEL: (212) 935 6900
FAX: (212) 935 4214
(OUT OF STATE CALL 1-000-272 7726)

CHARLES P. ROGERS
11134 ROCKVILLEPIKE
OPP WHITE FLINT MALL,
ROCKVILLE
MARYLAND, 20852.
TEL: (301) 770 5900

SHANNON TEAL,
1888 ILLINOIS STREET,
SAN FRANCISCO,
CA 94124.

SMITH & WATSON,
63RD STREET,
NEW YORK, 10021.
TEL: (212) 355 5615

WALTER WICKER INC.,
979 3RD AVENUE,
(15TH FLOOR),
NEW YORK.
TEL: (212) 758 0472